Trout from Small Streams

Trout from Small Streams

Dave Hughes

STACKPOLE
BOOKS

Published by
STACKPOLE BOOKS
5067 Ritter Road
Mechanicsburg, PA 17055
www.stackpolebooks.com

Printed in the United States

10   9   8   7   6   5   4   3   2   1

First edition

Library of Congress Cataloging-in-Publication Data
Hughes, Dave, 1945–
   Trout from small streams / by Dave Hughes.
      p. cm.
   ISBN 0-8117-0031-3 (hardcover)
   1. Trout fishing. 2. Fly fishing. I. Title.
   SH687 .H7647 2003
   799.1'757—dc21   2002007745

To my father, who taught me to fish small streams
by taking me to them,
letting them impart their own lessons.

CONTENTS

CHAPTER ONE

Land Shapes Water

How do you define a small stream? I've heard it said it's one you can jump across at the strictures. I agree that's small. As a definition it might work for a broad jumper, but it's frightfully narrow for me.

I picked up a recent book about fishing small streams. The cover featured a picture of the author wading what looked like a medium-size stream. I flipped the book over; it had a wraparound cover. The author was wading what I consider a big river. That's too broad a definition for me.

How do you narrow it down? Many folks say a small stream is one you can comfortably cast across. That comes closer, but before I accept it as a definition, I want to be sure you're as bad a caster as I am, at least for distance. I'll accept a definition that calls a small stream one that's a *short fly cast* across, since it suits my capabilities as a caster better than it does my abilities as a broad jumper.

A stream I can kneel next to, and easily cast across, might give me a sense of intimacy, a feeling that I can cover all of it without spoiling my own chances to take trout from any of it. But I occasionally fish what I consider medium-size trout streams that I can cover with an easy cast in their narrow areas, so let's add that *a small stream is a short cast across where the stream is at its widest*. Then perhaps we've got it, though as a definition it's still far from precise, because we all cast so differently.

The best definition of a small stream, I suspect, lies in that sense of intimacy rather than any distance you can jump or cast across. If you can work your way into a stream's watercourse, move upstream or down-stream along and even in it, and feel that you're a large and integral part of it, that you can observe and know or at least sense all of it from side to side, then that's small water.

Describing a small stream this way, as one that *feels* small to the person fishing it, is not nearly as precise as defining a small stream as one that's a certain width in feet, say five to ten feet across in the narrows and twenty to forty feet wide where its pools spread out. That would be as fine a definition as any. But I like latitude, and a lack of precision, in my own definition. I fish some streams that might be medium to others, with widths I'd have trouble casting across in sprawled-out places and currents that are substantially strong to wade against where they get gath-ered, but that still give me the feeling, when I'm inserted into them, that I'm a considerable part of them and can cover all of their water well, with short casts, from side to side. To me, that makes them small streams.

If I feel that I'm fishing a small stream, then that's defining it tightly enough for me. You'll have to arrive at your own definition. If we sat together on the bank of a stream, gestured at its parts, and debated about its size and the feeling it gave us about its size, I'm guessing we'd agree about it. Given that we agreed it was small, the *shape* of that stream might be almost astonishingly varied.

Up on the shoulders of mountains, small streams are most likely to be swift and tumbling, in a rush to get down to more level ground. Much of the best trout holding water will be in plunge pools hemmed in by boul-dered banks. In the foothills of the same mountains, small streams are less rushing. In places they'll display the riffle-run-pool structure of what are considered classic freestone trout streams, though in many small waters the run gets condensed out of the equation. Riffles plunge directly into pools. Down out of the hills and into the flatlands, small waters might be meandering meadow streams. They'll still have some riffles, runs, and pools, but much of the best holding water might be in sweeping bend pools, where currents carve depths beneath undercut banks.

All of these *mights* about the location of small stream types creep in because stretches of all of these types of water can be found along the course of any stream, at any elevation. You might even find all water types on the same small stream.

I grew up in the quarter-circle slice of geographic pie bordered by the miles-wide lower Columbia River to the north and the vast Pacific Ocean to the west. My father, two older brothers, and I fished the rain-forest streams that plunge out of the coastal hills of Oregon and enter directly into either the Columbia or the Pacific. In fall we trolled gangs of spinners for anadromous sea-run cutthroat trout in the estuaries of the stream systems. In winter we fished baits of eggs for steelhead that ascended some of the same streams. But our passion was summer dry-fly fishing for resident cutts, landlocked in small headwater streams where passage of anadromous fish was prevented by waterfalls.

Our favorite of these coastal streams was almost entirely of the forested foothill variety. Over eons it had eroded a somewhat gentle course through the typical sedimentary soils of the region, which was all ocean bottom uplifted twenty to thirty million years ago on account of a collision between an oceanic plate and a continental plate. When I first fished it, the watershed was heavily grown with hemlock and spruce; it has since been logged down to its death. Most of the stream descended through tall timber in a series of riffles and well-defined pools, over a bed of clean gravel and cobble. It was a typical foothill stream. It held cutthroat trout at an average of around ten inches long, including some fine and fat ones up to fifteen inches or so.

Four to five miles of foothill stream up from the waterfall that defined the downstream end of its trout fishing, a half mile or so of the stream, cut sharply through a lava flow. In some ancient past this lava had spewed out across what was then the ocean floor, before it was all raised up to form that slice of Oregon that I fished in my youth. Where the stream cut through this layer of hard basaltic rock, it was steep and tumbling, typical of a small mountain stream.

We called that half-mile stretch of stream *the gorge* because it was hemmed in by rock walls. In the gorge the holding water was a series of plunge pools flowing over and among great tumbled boulders. My brothers and I often left Dad down in the classic foothill water and hurried up to the gorge. We looked forward to reaching it and fishing through it, on our leapfrogging upstream sweep of the stream, because it held many more trout in all of its chopped-up, intricate lies than did the larger pools down below. Trout in the gorge were usually smaller than those in other parts of the stream, but when you're in your teens, action outgrows size.

At its upstream end this short, steep reach of mountainlike stream broke out abruptly into a long stretch of meadow stream that meandered flatly for a couple of miles. It did not take a geologist to recognize that this was caused by the same lava flow that formed the gorge. It had formed a natural dam, held the stream back for who knows how many millennia, shaping a long lake and allowing the deposition of alluvial soil, until the stream broke through, drained the lake, and eroded that quick descent for the half mile that we called the gorge.

This level meadow stretch of stream had been settled and farmed for a time, as all flatlands were when Oregon first got galloped into. When we fished it, beginning a decade after the end of World War II, a few abandoned farmsteads still stood along its course. The tall timber that crowded the rest of the stream was held back there by fallow fields, half grown over with briers and brush, grazed more by deer and elk than by a few feral cows.

This pastoral part of the stream was not our favorite for fishing because it wasn't suited to the bounding pace my dad, brothers, and I preferred to set. My mother loved it. Whenever she went out with us, she'd fish a few cutbanks and deep bend pools upstream from the car while the rest of us hiked far downstream through the timber on an overgrown railroad bed, left after the first logging at the turn of the century. Then my brothers and I abandoned Dad and helled back upstream. When we'd arrive, exhausted, she'd have just a few trout in her creel.

They would all be larger than any of ours.

Upstream from the meadow reach through the abandoned farms, the stream tipped up a bit and returned to its classical freestone character, through deep forest, and continued for a mile or so until it split. Neither of its branches was watered well enough to hold trout large enough to be legal. Making our decisions in those days based on the promise of water to provide trout for our creels, we never did bother to fish upstream from the fork.

This was my home stream until its watershed got logged while I was away at a later war. I won't get into the sadness of that, but I will say that the single stream, only a few miles long from the waterfall at the downstream end where its trout fishing began to the fork upstream where it ended, held the three types of small water you're most likely to find, wherever on this continent or in this world you fish small trout waters.

Small streams are shaped by their landscapes. They can be categorized roughly as *mountain,* bouldered and bounding; *foothill,* variously featured and somewhat civil; or *meadow,* if not meandering, at least peaceful. It is gradient, or steepness, that causes a stream to erode its course as it does. If the landscape is tilted, as it is in mountains and in parts of foothills as well, the water rushes and tends to draw fairly straight lines down toward larger rivers. If the landscape is less steep, as it is in most parts of the foothills, flows are still brisk, but the stream will have a slightly more serpentine course. If the landscape is nearly flat, flows are slower and streamcourses meander.

When the water is high in winter or spring, mountain streams tend to drive finer pebbles and gravel downstream, delivering them to the foothills. The bottom structure of mountain streams tends to be composed mostly of larger rocks and boulders. Foothill streams let the smaller stuff settle out. Their bottoms are mostly composed of gravel and cobble, the reason they're often called *freestone:* The stones on their bottoms tend to be loose. Silt is delivered downstream, usually to the larger and slower parts of river systems, but sometimes to meadow stretches interspersed along the course of a mountain or foothill stream. Meadow streams capture the finest gravel in their riffles, and in places have silt beds beneath their runs and pools.

Water in nature never dashes downhill without interruption, as it might in a pipe. No matter how steep or flat the inclination, it descends in steps. If it weren't for these steps, there would be few lies for trout. The steepness of a stream determines the shape of these steps.

Mountain streams tend to carve plunge pools, the water plummeting over the lip of a miniature waterfall or descending a short but brisk rapid or riffle. Pools tend to be short, their depths abrupt right at the head, fanning toward shallows at the lower end. If the entrance is a plunge, the water at the head will be frothed. If the entrance is a rapid or riffle, the water at the head of the pool will shape itself as a current tongue, flowing briskly down the middle, its energy dissipating as it goes along, with slower and calmer waters to each side.

If the pool is long enough, say ten to twenty feet or more, the plunge or current tongue will give way to a run, with constant depth and current speed, or perhaps even to a calm pool with some depth at its center. If the distance between drops is short, say just three to ten feet, the current might rush right through to the next drop, forming pocket water rather than runs or pools.

The most common type of holding water in a fast mountain stream is a riffle or plunge into a short but somewhat deep pool, then a quick uplifting and gathering of speed into a tailout. This tailout then enters the rapid, riffle, or tiny waterfall that descends quickly to the next step. Mountain streams also push occasional pools deep beneath the root balls of fallen trees and up against major or minor cliffs.

Almost always, right where the rushing water of a mountain stream enters a pool, you'll find tiny, still backwaters tucked behind the boulders at each side. Many of these are black on the surface and no bigger than a dinner plate. These eddies often appear to be too small to hold trout, and they're easy to miss. Never pass them up. They offer a pocket of sanctuary water situated right next to the current that rushes into the pool and thereby delivers food to trout. Especially in spring, when these tiny eddies might be the only calm water in the general rush of things, a big dry fly set onto such a tiny, calm spot in a mountain stream will elicit an almost instant response. My favorite fly for this work is a size 10 Stimulator, a golden stonefly imitation, since in spring a few of those large beasts are usually about, showing themselves recklessly to trout.

Any mountain step stretched out for enough distance to have a level run of water before gathering speed for the next drop will likely hold trout down its length. Wherever boulders interrupt the flow, or trenches drop the bottom a few inches to a foot or so, that will be the most certain address of a trout in the pool.

Small foothill streams, defined by gentler gradients and gravel and cobble rather than bouldered bottoms, will have more of what are envisioned as classic trout stream pools, though writ small. Water entering at the head of such a pool will be constricted and brisk, from a riffle or run. This narrow and fast current will form a current tongue entering into the pool, which slows as it moves downstream and loses energy. The pool itself will broaden out from this central current tongue, with the water on both sides slower and almost always shallower. Toward the lower end of the pool, the main thrust of water will lift up, begin to constrict, and flow more quickly until it reaches the run or riffle that delivers it down a step into the next pool.

The current tongue entering a classic small pool offers two things to trout. First, because of its erosional force, the deepest water in the pool will almost always be directly under the current tongue. That will make it the most secure lie in the pool, offering trout protection from overhead predation. Second, the current tongue is the delivery system for food that enters the pool. Most trout in a classic small pool will be located in proximity to that central current tongue, most of the time.

Not all foothill pools follow the prescribed plat. Many current tongues force their way under lodged root wads or fallen logs, and others turn abrupt corners or push along banks or even cliffs, forming deep side slots rather than center slots.

The upstream corners of small foothill pools, where the riffle enters and leaves pockets of soft water at the sides, are usually sloped and graveled rather than shouldered by boulders as they are in steeper mountain streams. They are often shallow and not as often sheltered eddies of peace in a passing turbulent world. But they form good lies at times because they allow a trout to take the uppermost position in a pool and, therefore, to get first shot at whatever the current delivers down to it. If any classic pool corner is deeper than a foot or so, giving protection from overhead predation and offering some sanctuary from the force of the entering current, at least one trout will usually hang out in that spot. You'll be able to catch it with a fly set there.

Small meadow streams have gentle gradients and slow flows. They tend to erode their safest depths along grassy undercut edges and around the outside curves of bend pools. They'll have more of a run-glide-undercut structure than the foothill riffle-run-pool nature. Any calm meadow water with enough protective depth can hold trout. But as in all kinds of small streams, trout tend to be found where current delivers food to them, and where they also find some sort of structure to break even a gentle current.

Meadow streams, as I use the term here, are defined by their low gradients and gentle flows, not by the source of their water. I emphasize this because the term *spring creek* is commonly used to describe the gentle type of water I'm talking about. Most spring creeks, because of their constant water levels and hence consistent erosion patterns, are meandering meadow streams in at least some sections. But let the landscape tip a spring creek down into a steep gradient, and it abruptly erodes its course into what we call a foothill or even mountain stream.

Mountain and foothill streams can have both freestone and meadow reaches. Spring creeks that arise as meandering meadow streams often enter steeper terrain and become bounding mountain or less boisterous foothill waters. The term *spring creek* defines the source of a system's water. The landscape still shapes the nature of the stream.

Land shapes water. And over geologic time, water shapes land back. Small streams erode their banks in different ways, thereby giving you an easy or difficult passage along them as you fish them and room or lack of it to work your casts over them.

Small streams that are subject to spate, whether from winter rainstorms or spring snowmelt, will push their vegetation back, uprooting during high flows whatever permanent growth might have tried to get a start during low flows. Most of the tree and limb detritus that drops onto the banks and into the water will be swept up, during high and heavy flows, and delivered down to the lower and larger parts of river systems.

Such spates, if violent, are brutal to trout. They can reshape favorite pools almost annually. But their forces can make your travel and casting along small waters a lot easier once the water drops to late-spring, summer, and early-fall fishing levels.

Annual spate flows also grade the banks, sloping them by tearing them down. This can shape them favorably for fishing. When high waters recede, you're not often walled in by high banks and tight brush. Instead, you often find convenient gravel bars alongside pools, on which to kneel and from which to launch a cast. That cast, depending on the degree to which your stream is subject to spate and therefore drives back vegetation, will encounter little or lots of interference from brush and limbs above and behind you.

One of the rainforest streams flowing out of my old corner of Oregon requires a day hike or long mountain bike ride on abandoned logging roads to reach. It's a steep stream, descending right off a mountain that stands high above the ocean. The view from the top end of the watershed includes waves not so far in the distance, detonating against volcanic intrusions near shore, where the stream enters the Pacific.

One of my favorite pools in this stream skirts the base of a cliff that stands about twenty feet high and drops straight to the water. When I boulder-hop up to the foot of this pool during low summer flows, I always hold fire with my dry fly and gaze up at the black side of that cliff. A few yellow monkey flowers and scattered patches of maidenhair fern have taken tentative root in cracks on the rock face. Most of them are far up toward the top.

The lower and middle parts of the cliff are swept bare of vegetation and reveal three distinct waterlines. The lowest waterline is where the stream laps gently along the bottom of the wall in summer, when I fish it, and therefore the only time ever see it. A second waterline, white and chalky on the dark basalt, is drawn distinctly along the cliff a bit higher than my head. This is the height of the average winter spate. Rainstorms here keep regular schedules during winter. Clouds arrive right off the ocean, heavy with water, settle against the mountain that forms the stream, and stop. They remain there and dump the bulk of their water load before they're light enough to lift up and move inland. This repeated brutality to the stream keeps its trout from attaining any great size. I never complain if the largest I catch in a day is less than a foot long, on account of the beauty of the tiny water from which I'm able to extract it.

The water likely reaches that middle waterline at least a few times each winter. I'd not like to be standing there when it did. A third water-line is etched across the cliff face perhaps ten feet above the second. It records the water height when an occasional extreme storm blows through. Weather forecasters call these hundred-year storms, though we seem to get them once or even twice in every decade. They leave trees, thicker than beams in buildings but snapped from their roots like twigs, skinned of their bark and stranded on hillsides at that highest waterline.

When I fish the stream in gentle summertime, these logs, some of them pitched precariously on high banks above the stream, seem far out of place. They are part of the strange beauty of that rainforest stream. But I'm able to navigate and fish the stream, and many others like it, more easily because these harsh storms beat the vegetation back, grade the banks, and deposit gravel bars from which I can cast.

Spring creeks, in contrast to spate streams, have relatively constant flows. They work their erosion at more steady levels. They don't rise up out of their banks and sweep brush and trees back. They carve their banks steep and sometimes abruptly deep, rather than sloped and shallow at the edges. Unless a spring creek is subject to at least minor rise and fall, it will not leave convenient gravel bars at bend pools. This is not to say anything bad about spring creeks. They're among the most beautiful small waters in the world, even in places where they're brushed in. But most of the photos you see of spring creeks with meandering weedy flows and manicured banks are pastorals. They involve the crop-pings of cows or the machinings of men.

Not long ago I inserted myself into the streamcourse of a south Wisconsin limestoner, a gorgeous little spring creek that held plump browns, some of which reached considerable size. The banks were grown to head-high grass and dropped off so abruptly, several feet down to the stream, that I had to sit and slide on the seat of my waders, digging my heels in for brakes. I arrived with a splash and had to wade upstream a couple of pools before I could start casting over any but frightened fish.

I stopped at a place where the stream straightened out into a deep, dark run along an undercut, just downstream from a gentle bend. My first backcast caught in the grass growing behind me, high overhead. I freed it and tried again, but I was in such tight circumstances that I got hung up again, lost my fly, and decided to hold my fire, assess the situation, and figure out how to get a fly to the water before I could ever figure out how to catch any trout.

The stream varied from three to five feet wide, its bend pools cut to depths in places almost equal to its width. Those meandering curves, obviously excellent lies for trout, were spaced twenty to thirty feet apart, which would have given me ample room for backcasts had it not been for the tall grasses that leaned in overhead from the high banks.

I was surrounded, armed with an 8½-foot rod, and realized at once why one of the most knowledgeable anglers in the area advocates stubby but delicate 5-foot rods. On this home stream of his, that's what it would take to keep backcasts beneath those damnable grasses.

I knelt and dropped my rod hand down next to the water, then cast with abrupt flicks of my wrist, a casting stroke that any fly-fishing school instructor would have scolded me for using. This low posture and quick stroke kept my backcast loop tight and low enough to get my Parachute Hopper out there where it could land on water. A trout came up and swatted it. Though it was not a big fish, I was able to bring it awkwardly to my hand, and in truth, I was quite proud about catching it.

I'd like to say that creative cast solved the stream for the rest of the day. But as I wended my way up the tunneled streamcourse, I continued to catch more grass on backcasts than I did trout on forecasts. The few trout I caught, some of which were big ones for where I was—fifteen-to sixteen-inch fish on that stream not as wide as my rod was long—were enough to keep me wading upstream far from grumpy.

But I stopped once, stood and straightened my stiff back, looked at the high banks and tall grass closing in tightly about me, and wished for the graded and cleared banks of my home spate stream, even with all its overhanging alder and conifer limbs.

CHAPTER TWO

Streams Shape Anglers

MY OLD HOME STREAM—THE ONE THAT, MORE THAN ANY OTHER, shaped me as an angler—I always viewed as frightfully choked by brush and trees. Now that I've fished small streams across this continent and on a few others, I recognize that it was quite open and friendly for a small stream.

It was in a conifer rainforest, and it flowed through encroaching alders. Its watershed was nearly mature, recovered from an earlier logging at the turn of the last century, if mature can be defined not as old-growth forest, but as forest grown enough to be ready to log again. An old-growth conifer forest is four hundred or more years old. But one that is fifty to sixty years old has already suppressed much of its undergrowth by choking off sunlight.

Where a stream slices a dark conifer forest, a line of light is let in, and that's where hardwoods such as alders grow. On my home stream, even those alders were old enough to be sufficiently tall that their over-reaching limbs linked fairly high overhead. Stray low limbs drooped into my backcast space and swept low enough to guard many pools against foreward casts. Mountain huckleberry bushes, while providing tart snacks, also crowded in to ensnare any errant casts. But the truth is, that stream and others that I fished in the area, all shaped by the same gradients and the same soft sedimentary soils uplifted from the ocean floor, allowed some room to cast.

I could kneel, gauge out a space before and behind me, flick a fly fore and back, and over most pools get the fly onto the water where I wanted it. If I screwed up by failing to calculate a cast before launching it, or to execute it accurately enough when I did, I'd hang up.

When I was young, in a hurry, handicapped by inexperience, by hand-me-down rods and lines not nearly balanced to them, I caught far more trees than I did trout. I can recall at times losing three or four flies in a row, sometimes all to the same limb that kept itself just out of reach above a beautiful pool, so that I was unable to rescue the ensnared flies; but I could not walk away from some beautiful bit of water without getting a fly onto it. Sometimes I became so vigorously angry that I'd have to sit down for a while and cool off before I could continue fishing without risk of breaking my rod or one of my own distal parts. I suppose, in that way—it's terrible to confess it—my home stream shaped not only my fishing, but my personality as well. I still have to sit down and cool off at times, and not just on trout streams.

I adapted, over many years, to the conditions in which I fished. I learned to kneel or crouch when I cast. I learned to at least glance at what was behind me before I tried to get a fly onto any water in front of me. I learned to keep my casting arm in close against my body. I learned to cast with such an abrupt flick of my wrist, not much more than a bump, that my rod arc was short and my line loop tight. I got good at it, I'll brag, but also was astonished when I discovered that the wonderful set of skills I'd learned on my small home streams were often handicaps when I branched out to begin fishing larger trout streams and rivers.

I was unable to cast very far. To this day, even after many years spent letting larger waters work on my skills, I've never become much of a distance caster. That's one reason I'm willing to accept a short cast across as one definition of a small stream. It suits my ability as a caster quite well.

I also became astonished, when my home stream was logged and its demise propelled me to explore others of many different types, to discover that I wasn't a very good small-stream fisherman except on my own home waters. My casting style was an asset on some small streams, a drawback on others. I could cast well, but only where I had room for forecasts and backcasts. Not all small streams have winter spates to beat back the brush and make room for unfurling line loops, even tight ones.

I had another, perhaps larger, handicap. I'd grown up with the idea ingrained that small-stream trout would take a dry fly, and if they wouldn't take that, then they'd take nothing at all.

I don't take full responsibility for that last mistake. It was wisdom passed down directly from my elders, especially my father. Looking back at the conditions that shaped him, it's not hard to understand the reason for that wisdom. When he learned to fly-fish, twenty and thirty years before he first took my brothers and me fishing, dry flies were at the center of things. Their use was held high, considered the only honorable way to take trout, in the magazines of the times.

Wet flies were on their undeserved fall into oblivion. Nymphs had recently arrived, but the methods that would allow them to be fished with some hope for success on small waters had not. Streamers never had or have been used much on small streams because most small waters lack room to cast a fly cross-stream and fish it down and around on the swing, the way streamers are typically fished. The same problem exists with wet flies, though wets, when cast straight upstream and fished dead-drift back down, or when cast, dangled, or dapped downstream, were used effectively on small streams before dry flies ever got invented.

These handicaps—my limited range of casting skills and dependence on dry flies—were solutions, not problems, on my own streams. But they restricted my chances to solve situations when I began fishing a wider range of small-stream types across the continent.

Each type of small stream—mountain, freestone, and meadow—calls for a separate set of dominant skills. If you're going to fish all of the stream types well, you need to hone all of your various fly-fishing abilities.

On mountain streams, your ability to wade bravely and safely, or to thread through brush without breaking your rod, to creep into casting position close and without revealing yourself or disturbing the water, added to your skill at making accurate casts the length of your leader and a short bit of line, most often while restricted by brush, will all add up to trout.

On classic foothill streams, with riffle, run, and pool structures, your ability to read water and pinpoint likely lies, then to place a fly precisely and drift it freely over or through that piece of water, will increase the number of trout you bring to hand. Those lies will often be tiny and protected by sweeps of deciduous limbs or conifer boughs. Such lies will coach you in casting while stooped or kneeling, sidearm, with a roll, sometimes even launching a forecast with no preparatory and measuring backcast.

Meadow streams call for an extension of all your skills at taking the right position and making the right presentation. But before you make any cast, they request that you make some extra observation, and observation becomes the critical skill in meadow stream fishing. You want to watch the water for some time before you approach it and drop your dry fly onto it or your sunk fly into it. Something might be going on, and that something might be your clue to the way to catch trout. Often it will be an aquatic insect hatch or fall of terrestrials and by holding back, at least briefly, you'll notice trout rising. Then you'll need to choose a fly that matches what trout are taking before creeping into position to present that fly in the way the natural it imitates might arrive in the sight of the trout.

It's best to back away from the idea that any of these sets of skills, though most useful on one stream type, is important only on that one stream type. Pools are so variously shaped, on all small waters, that any skill developed on one type of water can be applied to another. Observation, as an example, will add impact to your fishing on any small stream, not just a meadow stream. It took me a lot of years to recognize that some patient watching of the water would even increase my catch on my favorite forested coastal cutthroat streams, which I'd fished for so many years in such a hectic hurry. The realization struck as an epiphany on a day that sort of damns me.

It happened the summer I got back from Vietnam. Dad and I went out together, not to the home stream that had been moonscaped while I was gone, but to another local stream, still deep in timber. Mom had ordered up enough trout for a celebratory fry for the family, and in those days that stream could well afford to provide it. Not many other folks fished it, which is true to this day, though now when I fish it I release what I catch back into it. Back then I didn't always do that.

It was early July, the day was warm, and the shade of the trees, tall hemlock and spruce, felt good when we parked the car and dropped downhill on trails carved deep in the forest duff by the passage of generations of deer and elk. The stream, its voice muffled by all that excess of rainforest vegetation, murmured quietly as we approached it. Its classic little pools, bright in the riffles, dark where the water was deep, promised a perfect day when we tumbled down a steep bank and beheld them.

Dad assigned himself the upstream beat. He sat on a mossed boulder and rigged his Phillipson bamboo rod with its battered automatic reel, tied on a dry fly, and began fishing almost at once, from the point where we'd hit water. I backed away, struck an elk trail parallel to the stream, and hiked a half mile downstream before sliding down another bank, hitting the stream to fish up to where Dad had started.

I rigged and began fishing as quickly as Dad had. I'd thrashed through half a dozen pools before it occurred to me to notice that I'd not had a single rise to the size 12 Royal Wulff I'd tied on. That was not usual, on that stream, at that time. But it did happen on occasion that only a few small trout would take the white-winged Wulff, and it would become necessary to switch to a less showy Grizzly Wulff.

That's what I did, going one size smaller at the same time, returning to fishing with the expectation of sudden success. Nothing happened. I switched through a couple of other flies, a small Elk Hair Caddis and finally a big Stimulator, but still nothing. I was so surprised by this lack of success on any of my usual flies that I sat down at the foot of a pool to brood about it.

The pool where I sat was typical for a foothill stream: entered by a chattering white riffle, defined by a current tongue over some mild central depths that were darker than the water on both sides, ending in a tailout that gathered to rush into the riffle alongside which I had my stone seat. The pool had an alder tree leaning over it, white-barked in the sunshine, its limbs lofted twenty feet above the pool. It was a pretty pool, sure to hold at least one and likely two or three legal trout, though even on a good day if I caught one it would spook the others. But the prettiness and promise of the pool were not the main things I noticed.

What caught my eye, after just a few minutes of sitting and sulking, were a couple of quick but quiet rises far off to one side of the current tongue, in shallow and nearly still water not far from the bank, where I would not expect to see a trout. I moved into position in an instant and shot a cast up there. It covered the trout nicely. Covering a recent rise on a small stream usually ensures a fish on.

The big Stimulator I still had tied to my tippet drifted downstream on the slow current without any hint to the trout about how it got there. I was sure the trout would take it. Instead I saw an almost imperceptible welling up of water around the fly, just the slightest disturbance under it, but enough to tell me that the trout had seen the fly alight on the water, had driven over to have a look, had set its brakes before taking it.

This slight disturbance that marks a refusal, not as a by-the-way but as something to be emphasized as important, is your surest indication that it's time to change flies, whether you're fishing on a small stream or any other. I decided to do that but had no idea what fly to try next. So I watched the water another while first, which is what I should have done before ever rigging up.

The same trout rose to take something again, but clearly, now that I was watching more closely, without breaking the surface. I continued to watch but saw no insects on the water. While I concentrated on the surface out there, an insect helicoptered out of the forest and landed on my leg. I brushed it off and went back to watching the pool. Not until another landed on my hand and disturbed my concentration did I shift my focus to take a look at it. It was an alderfly, an insect type that begins life as a predaceous aquatic larva, migrates to damp streamside soil for pupation, emerges ashore and resembles a large black caddis as an adult. The winged adult flies around in June and July sunshine, attaches rows of eggs to leaves overhanging the water. When these eggs hatch, the larvae drop to the water, and the cycle begins again.

I looked up toward the trees and saw several more of the awkward adults flying around there. Most of them were in some state of descent toward the stream. Alderfly adults are poor fliers; they have trouble keeping altitude. Though I'd not seen an alderfly on the water, nor seen the trout take one, it all added up to what was happening out there in front of me. Alderflies are so blocky and heavy that when they lay their eggs on leaves over the stream, and lose their grip, they often fail to fly and fall to the water. When they do that, they almost instantly sink. Trout take them subsurface.

I had a few wet Alders in my box for use on small lakes and ponds, which is where I had always encountered trout feeding on adult alderflies. On stillwaters, during the midsummer alder fall, I'd long ago noticed that trout took the naturals after they'd subsided beneath the surface, not floating on top, and that it was necessary to fish for them with a wet fly, not a dry.

I'm hardly the first person to have noticed this about alderflies. Charles Kingsley's wet Alder, the one I had with me that day and still use to this day, was devised on Great Britain's Itchen River and was written about in 1878. It had and still has a peacock herl body, black hackle, and dark mottled turkey quill wings, all on a size 10 or 12 hook.

I tied one on, cast to that still edge water where I'd had the earlier refusal to the Stimulator, saw a bold swirl and my line tip jump. I set the hook. An autopsy of the trout that I led thrashing to my hand revealed half a dozen natural alderfly adults and nothing else.

The limit was ten trout back then. I always cleaned each trout the moment I caught it, wrapped each separately in a large salmonberry leaf, tucked it into a big outside pocket of the vest I wore. By the time I passed where Dad had started and continued on to catch up with him for lunch, I had my limit, almost enough trout for the dinner we'd been ordered to provide.

Dad had not gone far. I found him relaxing on a moss-softened boulder, already eating his lunch. I sat down near him, got out my sandwich, and asked him how his fishing had been. I had a pretty good guess, since it was he who had taught me that trout on small streams take dry flies or nothing at all.

"It's a strange day," Dad said. "I can't bring anything up."

"The same thing happened to me," I said.

"You didn't catch any either?"

"No," I said. "I caught a bunch on wet Alders."

He snorted at the idea, went on eating. I didn't say any more, but when we got up to decide between going on upstream and fishing some more or quitting, he noticed the buldge in my vest. The pocket was so full I couldn't get it zippered. Some salmonberry leaves and one or two trout tails stuck out.

"You do have fish!" Dad declared.

"I told you I did."

"What did you catch them on?"

I told him the truth again. He still didn't believe me until I pointed out all of the alderfly adults that had been landing on us, crawling all over us, that we'd been swatting away idly while we ate our lunch.

Then he accepted one of the wet flies, tied it to his leader, and worked the old Phillipson over just a few more pools before we had the requirements for dinner and hiked back up through the shade of the tall trees to the rig.

The type of small stream you start out on, and fish most often, will shape your primary set of small-stream skills. The water itself will hone your abilities; you don't have to pay conscious attention to the matter, though it might help.

If the stream is of the mountain sort, you'll become adept at creeping close, staying out of sight, casting short, dancing trout in abruptly. If you begin on a foothill stream, you'll get better and better at taking an unobtrusive position at the foot of a pool, assessing it for the most likely holding lies, making accurate casts, and getting drag-free drifts. If your early water is of the meadow stream sort, you'll get good at hanging back, making acute observations, then presenting your fly delicately when you've spotted some activity.

None of these skills is entirely separate and applicable on just one type of water. What serves you well on one type of small stream will work at times, and in certain sections, on all the others. To become a well-rounded small-water angler, adept on all water types, you need to develop the full set of skills that works best for each of them and is then transportable to all of them.

The best way to acquire those skills is to fish small waters as often as you can, in as many different places as possible, and let small waters of all types shape your various skills for you. Then in any situation you get into, you'll know precisely which ability to apply.

CHAPTER THREE

Gearing Down

WHEN MY DAD GETS OUT ON A SMALL STREAM, LESS OFTEN NOW IN HIS nineties than he used to, he still carries a large wicker creel. It is blackened by time and use, and it smells of trout kept and salmon eggs carried as backup against days when trout refuse to take dry flies. The creel is cumbersome. It works for Dad, because what we use for years and make work for us becomes what pleases us. If he were to replace that creel with a vest, chest pack, or belt bag he'd find each unworkable, even distressing, and he'd want his wicker creel back.

I tried one like his a few times when I first began fishing small streams. It banged around on my hip, got in my way, and I got rid of it in a hurry.

During almost all of my formative fly-fishing years I carried a canvas creel, looped by a strap over my right shoulder, adjusted to dangle at waist height on my left side. That's what I got used to, and it became what worked for me. But it had drawbacks that I was never able to solve.

The creel was divided into just two large compartments, one lined and waterproof for keeping trout, the other unlined for a terrible tangle of leaders, fly boxes, nippers, knives, pliers, line dressing, fly floatant, and on and on, all tossed in together because there was no way to keep them apart. Every time I needed some small item, I'd have to stop fishing and nearly empty the creel on a streamside rock or log to find what

I wanted. If I added a rain jacket and lunch for a long day on a stream, the creel would bulge on my hip, acquiring nearly fatal mass.

I recall fishing one early-summer day during what I believe was the last season for the canvas creel. I was finished with college and the army and old enough that lunch was habitually a baguette of bread, a small brick of sharp cheddar cheese, and a bottle of beer. That adds up to some weight.

I waded a tumbled reach of the small coastal stream that bounds off a mountain right into the Pacific Ocean. A day spent there contains as much rock-scrambling as it does fishing. The streamcourse is littered with car-size and sometimes larger boulders, most of them covered with thick beds of moss. Some are mossed and the moss then carpeted with candyflower creepers. In spring and summer it can look like the boulders themselves have burst into bloom.

The trunks of ancient alders that overhang the streambed are as overgrown with moss as the boulders beneath the leafy canopy the trees spread over the stream. Straight lines of licorice fern march up and down these massive, leaning trunks as if in military formation on important missions. The pools that work their way among the giant boulders beneath the forest canopy are deep, very dark, and somehow mysterious.

If you were ever going to encounter elves along a trout stream, this is the one where you'd find them.

I used to fish this remote stream alone a lot, in part because I desired to do that, in another part because my family and friends were too smart to want to go there. In truth, it is dangerous. In one place the streambed is so steep that it simply disappears down a whirlpool in a crack between boulders; it does not exit from a gap in this tossed bit of earth for one hundred nearly vertical feet.

The first time I fished up to this point and beheld the stream emerging from the earth, as if born there, I was astonished because I knew it was no spring creek. I scrambled up that hundred feet of tumbled rock and found the stream again, flowing almost flatly for a short way before resuming its ruggedness. I was relieved at its reappearance.

I was above this interruption to my own passage one day, in the fairly placid stretch, rock-hopping happily along from pool to pool, extracting trout as I went, benevolent to them all, letting them go back to the stream, when that damned creel, weighted with fishing gear and lunch, tossed me right off a rock. I'd taken a long leap to a small boulder in the middle of a pool. I landed in the center of the boulder, leaned forward to catch my balance, and the momentum of the jump swung my creel out in an arc away from my body. It was heavy enough to tug me into a quick spin, then a butt-first wallop into the water. The fish in that pool, which in a trout's lifetime were as likely to see an elf as an angler, had never seen anything happen like that.

After that wild ride, I started fishing small streams wearing the same vest I'd by then been using for years on larger trout waters. Vests accumulate mass of their own when they get loaded, which they seem to do no matter how you try to keep what you carry to a minimum. Mine caused some of the same problems as the creel. Because I used the same vest everywhere, on large streams and small, it always contained at least twice what I needed for any day on a small stream.

I discovered that I loved small-stream fishing so much, and came back to it so constantly even after my life accidentally got constructed in a way that allowed me to fish many of the famous fly-fishing Meccas of the world, that I got serious and outfitted myself specifically for trips to small waters. I put together a set of gear that is used there and nowhere else.

I began assembling this outfit with the theory that the only sure way to reduce the amount carried is to reduce the space in which to carry it. A vest gets filled because it has all those pockets and each pocket is examined to see what might fit in it. Something will be found for every pocket, from smallest to largest. In time any vest begins to bulge and probably should. I looked for some conveyance that would carry almost nothing, so I'd never have room for anything extra.

My first carriage specific to small streams, which could as well have been the final one because it worked very well for many years and still would, was an Orvis fishing shirt with a four-pocket front and a buttoned game pocket in the small of the back. This held plenty of gear for a full day on a small stream: lunch and rain jacket in the back, a couple of fly boxes, spare tippet spools, and all the small etceteras that I'll list later in the front pockets.

I wore out several of these shirts over many happy seasons on small streams, and nothing but the desire to experiment with other ideas drove me away from them. I still own one—I just trotted to the closet, got it out, and looked it over. It's fairly new, not used much, and could become what I use constantly again if it only had all of my small-stream stuff stored in its pockets.

That, in the end, is probably why I no longer use the shirt: I like to have all of my small-stream stuff kept in one small package, always ready to grab and go, but a shirt needs to be emptied out and washed once in a while, or it begins to smell as bad as Dad's old creel.

The next item I tried was a Wood River Sidekick II belt bag. It came with a shoulder strap, but I threw that away, strapped the bag around my waist, and used it exclusively for about fifteen years. It obviously worked, and still would. I have it next to me as I write this. It's worn to faded green, about 10 inches wide, 5 inches high, big enough to hold one large fly box or a couple of smaller ones. It has outside pockets for tippet spools, straps on the bottom for a rain jacket—enough places to tuck in or pin on all the little items needed on a day astream.

The bag has no room left for a sandwich if the fly box I carry is a big one. But I now carry a single box of medium size on small streams, so the bag has enough room for a small lunch, which is no longer a baguette of bread, a brick of cheese, and a bottle of beer. My small-stream lunch, like the other things I carry, has gotten smaller over all the years that I've fished them.

I became so confident in this bag and its constant contents that I once took a two-week trip to Chile, fishing some small streams but more large ones, without my vest. When packing for the trip I vacillated: Would I be balked at catching trout down there because I lacked something I needed? Would I get into situations I could not solve with so few things? I'd been there before and took an educated chance.

When I got to Chile and began fishing, I had everything that I truly needed. I felt liberated by the lack of burden and consequent increased mobility. I did a lot of hiking on that trip on a system of rivers and small tributary streams out in the Patagonian pampas. I don't know if I did all that hiking because I carried so little or carried so little so I could do a lot of hiking and exploring. These things get intertwined. But if you always carry a lot, you'll never cover much ground in comfort.

Covering ground is one of the many impulses that propel me up small streams. I cannot tell you precisely why, but I'm always eager to see what's around the next corner of any small stream I fish. This often keeps me from quitting when I know I should turn back. I know you share the same urge. I suspect it's an instinct, one I'd not like to place onto my modern list of discards. But some of the things I've seen on small streams might explain the urge as well as instinct.

I turned a corner of a tiny stream once and surprised a big bull elk with its head lowered to the river, inhaling a drink. It wasn't fifty feet from me. It didn't even take time to look astonished, as the many deer I've surprised the same way tend to do, jerking their heads up and looking at me wild-eyed before bolting, spray flying. That elk just exploded out of there. I can still see the bunched muscles in its haunches, the power with which it hit the high bank and blew up and over it, the hole it left in the water long after it left.

Another, more gentle time, far up the same stream where my old creel pitched me off a rock and into a pool, I climbed through a steep reach of stream and emerged onto a long, level bench in an alder patch. The trees were tall, straight, white-barked, with little moss and no marching ferns on their trunks. These alders stood like pillars over streamside ground that was grown to grass. No undergrowth grew there. Fallen logs had decayed, gone to moss, looked like great green caterpillars sprinkled about beneath the leafy alder canopy.

Against a massive first-growth stump, cut off at ten feet above the ground and almost the same in diameter, I found what was left of a cedar bolt cutter's lean-to. He'd erected his shelter over a recess indented into the stump. All that remained were a few pole stringers leaning against the stump, a wall he'd built up of stacked logs, now crumbling, and a toilet seat that he'd packed in to give himself a comfortable seat from which to gaze over that gorgeous glade and the stream gliding through it.

The shelter had been abandoned for at least forty years before I found it. Whoever made it had probably gone on by then, died in the last great war or of old age. I've been back just once in ten years; that stretch of stream is too difficult and dangerous to fish often. But it's the kind of discovery that both draws and drives me around corners of small streams, wherever in the world I fish them.

The less you carry, the more corners you can turn and the more things you can discover. It's probably not peripheral that the more water you can cover, the more trout you can catch.

I retired my Sidekick II belt bag just recently, not because it failed in any way, but again out of desire to try something new. Different tricks for reducing gear are now coming on the market faster than any angler will ever be able to try them all. They include belt packs, chest packs, harnesses with chest packs in front, belt bags below, and daypacks in back. Some fishing daypacks have hydration chambers. You sip water through a tube draped over your shoulder, presumably without the need to miss a single casting stroke. As the great angling essayist Ted Leeson recently wrote, most anglers still drink water rather than rehydrate themselves.

All of these new ways to carry gear will work for some and not for others. One of them will be best for you. Unlike me, you might just like to wear the same vest on small streams that you use in all your other fishing. My guess is that's what most folks do, with good reason. A vest often contains more than is needed for a day spent fishing a small stream. But it rarely lacks any item that's needed.

The belt bag I'm using now is from Japan, made of sturdy canvas, has both shoulder and belt straps. It is a bit smaller and a lot prettier, but otherwise it looks almost exactly like the canvas creel I used when I started fishing small streams more years ago than I care to count. It has a zippered closure, less convenient than the Velcro-fastened top flap of the Sidekick II. It has more room inside for fly boxes and a sandwich.

The new bag has such an intricacy of inside and outside pockets that I sometimes have to shake everything out on a streamside rock or log to find the item I'm after—the same problem I had with my earliest creel, but for the opposite reason: not a tangle of things thrown together, but such a mystery of things stored separately that I can never remember where I put them. But that's just a matter of getting used to it. I've been using this bag for just a couple of seasons. It hasn't become a part of me yet, but it will. It takes time, and I've got it to give it.

I use this beautiful bag not because it works better than anything else I've used, but because I've gone back to fishing bamboo rods on small streams. The canvas bag, which so resembles my original creel but is so much more usefully designed, looks better with bamboo. That's all. But that might be a way to avoid confessing I'm getting older as I go along, and the new bag reminds me of my lost youth spent rock-hopping up small streams with a canvas creel flying about me. If that's the real reason, it's good enough for me. I still spend more time fishing small streams than I do any other kind of angling. But I keep the new bag belted loosely at my waist, so it does not threaten to throw me off rocks.

The contents of this bag and all its predecessors begin with a fly box filled with flies specifically chosen for small waters. This box is so important it has a separate chapter that comes later. Next in importance are spare tippet spools in 3X, 4X, 5X, and 6X, along with a couple of store-bought leaders 7$^1/_2$ feet long, tapered to 3X. That gives me the options of fishing a stout 3X leader about the length of the rod I carry, for size 8 and 10 flies, or, far more often, adding a 2-foot tippet of 4X and fishing a leader just that much longer than the rod I use on small streams, for size 12 and 14 flies.

If desired, I can tie in a foot of 4X, then add a 2-foot tippet of 5X, for fishing size 14 and 16 flies. If I'm on a small meadow stream, a hatch of size 18 or 20 insects is on, and trout are fussy, I can taper down to a 6X tippet. By using a base leader the length of the rod and adding tippet sections as conditions demand it, I'm making a leader that is both finer and longer at the same time, which is the correct formula for taking small-stream trout, or any other trout, as they get more selective and the situation becomes more demanding.

It took a lot of years to arrive at this simple leader formula. For many years I tied my own leaders, in a wide variety of lengths and tippet diameters, to cover all sorts of situations on small streams, larger moving waters, and stillwaters as well. Then I discovered I was doing most of my fishing with one leader butt affixed to the line for days or even weeks, adjusting midtapers and tippets to suit different situations.

One day I sat in the grass alongside a small Montana spring creek, pulled out a new hand-tied leader to cast over a hatch of tiny mayflies, and found that the carefully tied tippet had deteriorated with age before it got a chance to get into action. I tucked it back into the vest to discard later, rebuilt the leader that was already on my rod, with fresh tippet that was already in my vest, and went back to fishing with sufficient success to satisfy me.

Not much later I discarded most of the specific leaders I'd tied and with them the idea that I needed a different leader for every situation. Now I buy 7$^1/_2$ foot leaders as the base for all of my small-stream fishing and 10-foot leaders upon which to build what I need for most medium and large streams. Part of this is laziness, but I don't think I'd get any better results with leaders tied by hand.

Another misadventure I had with leaders might be instructive. It happened when I was young enough to believe everything I read about fishing but not experienced enough, or smart enough, to interpret what I read as it applied to my own fishing. A famous fishing writer, who apparently fished insect hatches over fussy trout on spring creeks, wrote that he no longer fished leaders shorter than 15 feet and that at least a full third of that was always tippet. I instantly recognized my mistake, fishing 7- to 9-foot leaders on my tiny home streams. I tied up half a dozen leaders that were about twice the length of the rod I would use to cast them.

There's no reason to dwell on the difficulties this caused the next time I fished my favorite small stream. It was a frustrating day. I spent the first half of it blaming myself for not being good enough to handle those proper leaders. Then I crept close to the foot of a short pool from which I'd often taken nice trout in the past.

I knelt, calculated the backcast that had to stay low beneath some sweepers and stop short of branches only about ten feet behind me. I pulled the necessary length of line from the reel and discovered that the cast, with that long leader, was not going to need any line at all. I attempted to launch the cast with nothing but leader beyond the rod tip. The entire length of it accordioned onto the water just beyond my wadered toes, with the fly sitting daintily atop the pile. No trout was ever going to rise to take that fly.

I almost laughed at my own gullibility as I sat down on a streamside rock, overhung by tree limbs, and truncated that leader to a third of its original length. I tapered the remaining stump of it out to the length of my fly rod. Then it fished fine. I continued upstream, extracting trout as I always had: on casts of ten to around thirty feet, some with just a little line out, but always with enough line in the air to transfer the speed of the rod tip through to the leader butt and down a quick taper to the fly.

I'll offer a couple of important admonitions about leaders. Buy base leaders and tippet spools of the same brand, or they'll be weak wherever you join them with knots. Buy a fresh set of leaders and tippet spools at the beginning of each season. Modern leader materials weaken with age. I'll give you an example of what can happen, if you fail to use fresh material, that does not sit well with my wife.

Masako and I fished a small stream that hurries off the forested east slope of the Cascade Mountains in Oregon and flattens out when it reaches the almost arid flatlands. It meanders through some long pools there and holds some outsize trout before dashing down a canyon and into the Deschutes River. We'd been fishing hoppers on the placid part of the stream without much success, and we arrived at a pool that was bouldered at the head and flowed down in even depths for fifty feet or so before passing under an alder tree that draped branches low over the water.

It was Masako's turn to fish the water first. She asked me what she should do, in light of the lack of luck on drys. I suggested she drop a beadhead nymph off the stern of the hopper she already had on, on a couple feet of 4X tippet. She batted her eyes and asked if I minded doing it for her, a mistake she's made less often after what happened next.

I was wearing my vest that day, instead of my small-stream belt bag, because we'd been fishing the Deschutes earlier. I'd worn the vest over there, and I didn't take time to dig in my wader bag for the little canvas creel before we began fishing the smaller tributary. I'd worn the vest seldom that season and had neglected to refresh the set of tippet spools, 3X through 7X, that I always kept in one of its front pockets. I spooled off 2 feet of 4X, tied it to the bend of Masako's grasshopper hook with an improved clinch knot, then tied a size 14 Olive Beadhead nymph to the other end of this tippet with the same knot.

Masako angled a nice cast in above those overhanging tree limbs. And the grasshopper floated toward them and was about to pass beneath them when it suddenly popped under the water. She set the hook. A portly rainbow, about eighteen inches long, shot into the air and almost tangled itself in the branches, landed with a smack, and tore off up the pool. As the fight went along, Masako developed an increasing desire to get a photo of herself, smiling and holding up that fat trout, to send to her friends in the fishing club she still belongs to in Tokyo. They don't catch many that shape and size over there.

It was a long fight, and she'd almost worn the trout out, when it got to the far side of the pool where the water shallowed up. The trout wallowed over there, and the leader suddenly parted. Masako didn't feel that she'd applied any undue pressure. She reeled up, got ahold of that tippet I'd tied on for her, and gave it a quick tug. It popped without much force. I got an unfriendly look.

She replaced it with tippet of her own, dangled another beadhead, was able to hook and land a bigger trout without any help from me. I was relieved to take her photo with it. Now I write the date on the package of a base leader or tippet spool whenever I buy a new one and replace them when they get any older than a single year.

Having learned in opposition to early instruction that small-stream trout will indeed take nymphs, rather than nothing at all on days that they refuse to take dry flies, I always carry the means to fish nymphs shallow or deep. I prefer yarn indicators over hard ones, though I have no solid reasons for that and don't give it out as advice. You need strike indicators of some sort. I knot a hank of yellow polypro yarn to an out-side D-ring of my belt bag, and snip indicators from it as I need them.

You could as well carry a couple sizes of hard indicators. In some small-stream situations, where the water is fast and forceful, a couple of pliable stick-on indicators, separated on the leader by a foot or so, let you detect leader movements in opposition to the current, a prediction that a trout has taken your weighted nymph down below. I also carry nontoxic split shot, in a little rotary container, in sizes BB, #1, #4, and #6. This gives me some options for getting nymphs close to the bottom in water of various depths and current speeds.

My kit contains a bottle of paste floatant for dry flies and a pad of pretreated line dressing. I consider it important to clean my line before beginning to fish each day. It's a way to slow down, get a feel for the stream and for the day before rigging and starting to fish. It's also a way to improve my fishing. We tend to put such confidence in modern coated lines that we often neglect to clean them. You'll be surprised how much better your casting becomes if you clean your fly line once a day. You might also be surprised how much better your fishing becomes if you take a few minutes to observe conditions while cleaning your line, before plunging in to fish a small stream.

The main tool in my bag is a hemostat with scissor blades behind the jaws. The long, flat points are used to debarb any hooks I've neglected to pinch down before tying the fly, and to release trout. The scissors cut yarn indicators. I keep a pair of leader nippers on a zinger—a retractable cord—pinned to the outside of the bag. I carry a nail knot tier in the bag. I rarely use it, but it's frustrating to do without one when, on account of some disaster, you need to tie a new base leader to your line tip. I carry a small Swiss Army knife with a single sharp blade, tweezers, and scissors, because it's never smart to be out in the woods without a knife for emergencies, and small streams are almost always out in the woods.

A cigarette lighter and fire-starter cubes are a necessary part of my own equipment, always tucked in my bag, but it's possible I get into more remote situations than you anticipate. The small streams I fish are typically at least a little isolated, or I might not want to be there. A dunking is never more than a slight slip away. I don't want to wonder if I'll be able to start a fire if I ever need one. I've not often had to have one, but I've often enjoyed building a fire and sitting by it, sometimes even cooking over it, alongside a small stream.

I always knot an old handkerchief to the outside of my bag, to wick away excess moisture and fluff up a dry fly after it has taken a trout. I also use the handkerchief to rub out excess floatant when, as usual, I overapply it and mat my fly into a mess.

I carry a few items that reflect my personal curiosity about the insects that trout eat. I always carry a small jar lid, painted white inside, in which I can place the stomach contents of any trout I might kill for a streamside lunch. Add water to the stomach contents in this jar lid, stir gently, and whatever the trout has been eating will be revealed. I also carry a small aquarium net to capture live specimens out of the air or off the surface of the water. A magnifying glass in 4X to 6X is excellent for a closer look at whatever is found. A couple of 1-dram vials filled with alcohol and the tweezers on the Swiss Army knife allow me to collect any specimens I might desire to take home to the tying bench.

That's all of it.

It's a pretty short list of items to carry, which is why I can get it all into a tiny belt bag. The list covers all of my needs and most of my wants for a day spent on a small stream. It's critical, if you fish small streams often and want to enjoy them when you do, that you keep whatever vest, belt bag, or creel you choose constantly stocked. If you move fly boxes, tools, or trinkets back and forth between the small-stream outfit and the fishing vest you wear on larger waters, you'll get out on a small stream sometime soon and discover you've left something important at home.

Maybe I should mention that I've recently designated a specific reel for small-stream fishing. I won't describe the day that caused me to do that; none of it involved fishing. I've armed the reel with a line balanced to my favorite small-stream rod and now keep it permanently stored in my small-stream bag.

I keep this belt bag constantly packed and ready to go, stored in a daypack, along with waders, water bottle, rain jacket, flashlight, travel binoculars, and a few not minor items such as toilet paper, sunscreen, and mosquito repellent. These are the kinds of things that are needed on some streams some days and not on others. The daypack itself is also stored stocked and always stands ready for a trip. It usually rides around in the back of my pickup.

The last trip I took with that daypack was to Ireland. With the addition of a few extra fly boxes, two seven-piece pack rods, reels to match, and a pocket camera with a Zeis lens, it contained everything I needed for fishing.

It was a writer's junket. Every time the group I was with headed out from a lodge to a stream or lake, I'd take only that daypack, and I'd get asked by the gillies, "Where's your fishing gear?" It was all there, and I don't recall lacking anything.

Waders are the most difficult thing to get into a daypack, though they can always be rolled and tied to the outside. Because of my over-riding desire for compactness, I now use breathables, boot-footed and felt-soled, which roll up into their own stuff bag and take little space. But I think that's a mistake. Those rubber boots aren't always enough protection for my feet on small streams. At the end of a day on a rocky mountain stream, I'm footsore and hobbling. For such waters, it's hard to beat sturdy felt-soled brogues.

It's also hard to beat felted hip boots with firm foot protection and room for an extra pair of thick wool socks. The socks are more for padding and protection from rocks than they are for warmth. My main problem with hip boots is forgetting I'm not wearing waders. When I squat to release a trout, I dip my tail into the water.

Out of forty years fishing small streams, I'd guess that I've spent ten years wading wet, twenty years wearing hip boots, and the last ten years wading wet when the water is not too cold and wearing breathable waders when they're needed. Wading wet at first meant gluing carpet to worn-out tennis shoes, then later, when I could afford it, ordering a new set of felt-soled canvas wading shoes at the beginning of every other season or so. They'd wear out in a season, open up the length of the seam on the inside of the arch, let in so much bottom gravel that I'd have to slice the outsides open to give the gravel a way to get out. It's better to use sturdy felt-soled brogues to protect your feet from bruising when wading wet.

The best hip boots I've worn have felt soles, sturdy rubber feet, and canvas uppers. The pair I keep in the back of the rig for emergencies, and still wear on small streams a few times each season, is at least fifteen years old. They've been almost bulletproof over all those years, which can't be said about breathable waders. Breathables cost two to four times the price of a good pair of hippers and are good for just a few seasons, depending of course on how often you use them and how many brush and brier patches you thrash through in them.

If I were on a budget and investing in an outfit strictly for small streams, I'd risk dipping my bottom and buy hip boots. Otherwise, I'd buy breathables and brogues. Then I'd be outfitted to wade wet when I wanted and dry when it seemed smarter.

CHAPTER FOUR

Rods

SMALL STREAMS ARE FUN AND SO ARE FLY RODS, BUT IT'S NO FUN thrashing around on a small stream with the wrong rod. Fly rods should not be at the core of our thinking about fly-fishing tackle, but they are. They're the animated part of our gear. They move. They perform. They feel good or feel bad. Some are beautiful and others look like clubs, though those that look bad can feel fine and perform well, whereas those that look so wondrous that they ignite a gleam in the eye can fish as badly as baseball bats.

Lines, not rods, should be at the core of any discussion about fly tackle selection for small streams or any other kind of fly fishing. The line transfers its energy to the leader, turns the leader over, and sets the fly onto water. If the line is too heavy, the fly lands with a smack. If the line is too light, the leader fails to extend itself and lands on the water in a pile, with the fly set on top. But the line weight that will deliver one size fly perfectly will not work as well with another that is either larger or smaller. That means that neither fly rods nor fly lines—instead, flies themselves—belong, if not at the center of any discussion about fly-fishing tackle, at least at its beginning.

Trout in small streams eat quite a variety of foods. They do not often see one insect species, or any other single food form, in such abundance that they get selective about it, though if they do focus on one item they can suddenly and surprisingly be just as snotty about fly pattern as trout in a stream of any other size. It's not that small-stream trout, or any others, refuse to take your fly because it doesn't look exactly like what they're busy eating at the moment. It's that they're so satisfied with what they're eating, and so focused on it, that they don't recognize any fly that fails to look like it as food at that instant. Take away the abundant food source on a small stream, and those same trout will be willing to take a broader array of patterns, so long as what you show them has some resemblance to something they've been eating recently.

Our discussion here is broadly tackle selection, and narrowly rods, so we're less interested at the moment in imitation than we are in fly size. The average size fly you'll want to cast predicts the proper line weight to turn over both leader and fly, which ultimately informs rod selection.

Most of the bites that trout eat in small streams are insects, either aquatic or terrestrial. Trout do feed on big and satisfying meals such as crayfish, dace, and sculpins, and you might occasionally want to imitate them. But most of the time you'll cast flies at the center of the size scale of water and landborne insects.

Most of your small-stream fly fishing will be done with size 12, 14, and 16 flies. When trout see big stoneflies in spring, especially on boisterous freestone streams, they will be susceptible to large size 8 and 10 patterns such as the Stimulator. When trout feed on hatching midges or falls of tiny beetles or ants, they'll take flies at the smaller end of the scale, usually sizes 18 and 20, and refuse all others.

These insects at opposite ends of the size spectrum, along with many others such as big grasshoppers and tiny Trico mayflies, are exceptions. The small-stream rule is that trout eat insects in the medium range of fly sizes: 12 to 16. Most of the flies you cast over small waters should reflect those most common food sizes. Many will be dry flies that are modestly to heavily hackled for flotation. Others will be nymphs weighted so they'll sink.

Lines that deliver bushy dry flies in these medium sizes and turn over nymph rigs fall in a narrow range from 3-weight at the lightest to 5-weight at the heaviest. Though I've heard the argument for delicate 2-weights and even modern 1-weights for the small trout we think of most often as being small-stream fare, to me these are specialty lines for fishing tiny flies over visible feeding fish on the runs and flats of larger streams and rivers, often spring creeks and tailwaters. 1- and 2-

weight lines are too light to turn over the average range of dry flies fished on small streams, at least with any authority. Most of the rods designed to fish light lines are too soft, flex over too much of the full rod length, to deliver the tight, controlled loops often needed to thread needles in small-stream fishing. Leave these lightest lines for use on larger waters.

Heavier 6- and 7-weight lines will obviously boss small-stream flies around, but they'll do it with a bit too much emphasis, setting them onto the water with a smash. Even if you're able to deliver the fly with some delicacy the line itself will be thicker and, therefore, will land with more impact and be more visible on the water than necessary. Most modern rods designed for such lines are distance-casting tools. They're stiff for most of their length, difficult to load with just a little line out and, therefore, difficult to control on a short cast.

Control is what you're after in small-stream fishing, and lines in the 3-, 4-, and 5-weight range are what hand control to you best at the ranges you'll be casting, with the fly sizes you'll be using.

The 4-weight line is at the center of that favorable range and is my favorite for small-stream fishing. The 3-weight is a little light to boss around the brushy flies that exceed the upper end of the average: size 8 and 10 Stimulators and Parachute Hoppers. I fish those, or use them as platforms from which to dangle beadhead nymphs, often enough that I own a couple of very nice 3-weights but fish them most often on larger waters.

I consider the 5-weight line excellent but just a bit more than is needed to boss small-stream flies around. I own several rods for that size line but most of them are $8^{1}/_{2}$ to 9 feet long, for fishing larger waters, though not necessarily with larger flies.

I use double-taper floating lines almost exclusively for small-stream fishing and recommend you at least try one if you are already armed with a weight-forward. The double-taper has a slightly longer front taper and is therefore a bit more delicate. More of the weight-forward line's weight is stacked in a shorter forward section; hence, it loads the rod better for the short casts that are typical on small streams.

You will never cast beyond the fat portion of a weight-forward line, so mending and line control are not an issue. It might come down to which line balances your rod best and handles best on a short cast and how much delicacy you desire. For me, the right line for a small-stream rod is usually a double-taper line one size heavier than that recommended by the rod manufacturer. If a weight-forward works better for you on your rod, use it.

To my mild dismay in my striving over the years toward the perfect small-stream fly rod, I've arrived at the desired 4-weight rod, but it casts a 5-weight line.

Let me describe some of my strivings.

My first fishing rod started out as an 8-foot bamboo fly rod before somebody older than me in the family—everybody in the family was older and, through some extraordinary law of life, continues to be—broke about 8 inches off its tip and handed it down to preteen me. I used it to lob split shot and baits of single salmon eggs scant feet into pools almost at my feet. The rod worked for that, which means it worked for me for years. But its cheap and wobbly reel was spooled with heavy monofilament, not a fly line.

Sometime in my early teens, for some reason I cannot recall, I suddenly decided to become a fly fisherman. My Dad was one, and still is, though back then his condition was intermittent. If trout wouldn't rise to his dry flies, he'd join us boys, nip off his fly, tie on a gold single-egg hook, pinch a split shot to his leader with his teeth. Then he'd thread a bleeding salmon egg or two to that hook, lob it out, and let it sit just like we did.

But that's an oversimplification. What we did was read those current tongues, get up alongside them as close as we could, drop our tiny baits in at the head of them, loft our rods, and encourage those eggs to tumble along the bottom, right down the current slot. It was a fairly precise prediction of some of the best small-stream nymph fishing I would have in my future, though I had no idea about that at the time.

I'm guessing I contracted my desire to take up fly fishing from watching Dad work magic with his old Phillipson bamboo and some brushy dry flies over beautiful pools. It was always in sunshine because he liked to fish dry flies on bright days. I always watched from a distance. When Dad fished dry flies he required my brothers and me to stay well behind him, which caused us to fish the water second, which is probably why we got into the habit early of dividing any stream into beats and separating, each to fish his beat by himself. I have an antipathy, to this day, to fishing water that's already been cast over.

For a fly line with which to arm that foreshortened rod, I stepped with Dad into the dark garage of one of his friends, who rummaged through an abandoned tackle box tangled with wooden salmon plugs and rusted hooks, spoons, and spinners until he found a fly line and extricated it from the tangle, of which it was an interwoven part. I paid a dollar for it and went home eager to cast it.

At that time, in my narrow scope of knowledge, a fly line was a fly line. There were no 3-weights, 4-weights, and 5-weights; that advanced system would be devised later. There were HEHs, HDHs, and HCHs. My question to Dad's friend about which this line might be got the response that it would be just right for the rod I was using, which turned out not even nearly true.

The line was a level H, about what would now be a 4-weight. The truncated rod might have been balanced by a 6-weight before it lost its delicate tip. It required a lot heavier line than that when I tried to learn to cast it with that thin level twine.

I worked at it in the backyard every night after school, and my chief recollection is of enormous frustration. One night when Dad came home from work, I begged him to give me a lesson. He would not, and I held that against him for many years. Not until a long time later did I realize that he'd refused because he'd learned he knew about fly casting on his own, simply by going fishing and thereby casting, and had no idea how to teach anybody else. I believe now that he did me a favor but that's not what I thought at the time.

I became able to get a fly a short way with that rod and line, and tried fly-fishing with it on streams around home. I'd like to retell the wondrous and shining epiphany of my first fly-caught trout, but I can't remember a thing about it. All I can remember is a continuation, onstream, of the frustration I'd suffered in the backyard. Streams had trees around to catch, and trees are what I caught.

I went back to lobbing baits of single eggs until I got a summer job shoveling mink droppings at a dollar an hour and saved enough money to order a rod from Herter's. It was 7½ feet long and made of fiberglass. Hyperbolic catalog copy announced that it was balanced perfectly to an HDH line, so I ordered one along with it. That copy wasn't true by a line weight or two, but the rod and line were a lot closer match than what I'd been using. My conversion to fly fishing became complete with that outfit.

It served me for several youthful years of scrambling along my home trout streams. I thought it was fine, though if I were to pick it up now and cast it, I'd toss it aside disdainfully and declare it a noodle, which it was. That's why, to this day, I warn you to avoid soft rods of any weight for small-stream trout fishing. They fail to create tight line loops and control short, brisk casts.

That Herter's rod got into lots of adventures, most of them because my felt soles were always worn down and slick in those years. I kept falling down and breaking it. Most times I could fix it myself, with some shrinkage, but not always. The first new tip I ordered matched the old butt and cast the same as the original. The next new tip was a different color than the original, and also softer, so the rod became two-tone and more of a noodle. When that last off-color tip got broken, Herter's wrote back that they no longer made that model rod and had run out of replacement tips for it.

That Herter's rod, the first somewhat-but-not-quite-balanced outfit I ever owned, delivered me along small streams for five or six years, right into my college years.

Just after the Herter's rod was declared dead, a distant uncle passed on as well. My aunt gave me a fly rod that had been standing neglected in his closet for some years. It was $8^1/_2$ feet long, hollow fiberglass, three-piece, bright white. I armed it with the line that had survived the Herter's rod, stepped out into the backyard, made one cast, and the center section snapped just above the lower ferrule. I took the rod into the garage workshop, removed the broken glass from the inside of the ferrule, used a hacksaw to even the end of the center section just above the break, glued the ferrule back to it.

It snapped in the same place on the next cast.

I repeated the repair, and the center section of the rod broke again. In frustration, I threw the center section away and jammed the tip section into the lower ferrule. The female end of the ferrule still had the broken fiberglass inside and was, by accident, the right size to accept the male end of the tip ferrule. With the tip section affixed directly to the butt section, the result was a few inches short of 6 feet long and had an ugly step at its midpoint but did not break when I took it back into the yard to cast it.

This remains of a rod did not get loaded properly until I got a remarkable length of that light line into the air. The tip worked, but the butt did not even begin to bend. Everybody in the family came out to watch me cast it and laugh, as they might have done had I taught the unruly family dog to sit up and beg.

I ordered a GBG line—about an 8-weight—from dependable Herter's and fished that truncated rod for two summers. At first it was an accident when a fly landed on water near where I wanted it and with less than a violent splash. Prowling small streams with it felt a little like hunting trout with a big-game rifle. I frightened far more fish than I caught. But I slowly learned how to fish with it, and I slowly developed an affection for it. I put it away carefully in the attic when I went to Vietnam. It went missing, just like my home stream, while I was over there.

I still long for that rod, would like to find it in that attic and fish it once more, to this day.

I commanded an isolated communications site in the Mekong Delta, though the word *isolated* overdramatizes it. The site had its own perimeter, but a Navy gunboat base and 9th ARVN division headquarters were near enough if not to provide security, then at least to furnish more enticing targets. Nights in my hot hooch I read novels and, whenever I could get one, a *Field & Stream*. Toward the end of my tour, I saw an ad for an exciting new thing called an Orvis catalog. I had one sent.

When the catalog arrived, I wore it out looking at the photos of fly rods. These set off visions of my home stream, which I was not aware was having its watershed chewed up by chain saws while I dreamed about being there. I'd close my eyes, lie back in my bunk, wish I was sitting idly on one of the stream's gravel bars, in sunshine, surrounded by foxglove flowers, overhung by alders, listening to a riffle's bright song or a run's soft voice. I didn't dream about fishing so much as I dreamed of just sitting there, lazing, looking, with nothing that needed to be done. That catalog became my ticket to that vision. As a marketing strategy, it must have been a success even to those not caught on the wrong side of the world, at least in trout-fishing terms, because Orvis is now a giant.

I looked at the photos of bamboo rods and longed for them. I spent hours in pleasant internal debate about which would be best for the small streams I fished. Not long before leaving, I astonished my frugal family by sending Orvis a check, but not for bamboo. I ordered a fiberglass Full-Flex small-stream rod, $6^{1}/_{2}$ feet long, complete with a double-taper, 6-weight line, and a reel to hold the line plus 50 yards of backing. It would be the first balanced outfit I ever owned. The check was for $75.

When I returned to the States, my father told me I was foolish to spend so much money on a fly rod. I countered, mathematically, that he owned a thousand-dollar trap gun that he didn't fire a thousand times in a season; that if I fished a mile of trout stream, I'd cast the rod more times in a day than he'd shoot his shotgun in a year. I didn't get anywhere with that argument, but I did bolt out to my home stream almost the instant I got back.

It was moonscaped, but there were others.

I didn't just sit on gravel bars alongside them, in accordance with my distant vision. I blew up streams more swiftly than I ever had in my past. I couldn't be held back from seeing what was around next corners. I was released. I was a torrent.

That short Orvis rod, almost as stiff as a pool cue but armed with a line heavy enough to balance it and get it bent, was the perfect transportation up those tiny rainforest streams. I caught fish; I even counted fish; some days I caught a lot. Most times out I killed at least a few of them. Some times out I killed a limit of them, enough to bring home to feed the family.

I had no trouble getting used to that short, stiff rod because the truncated one I'd been using before leaving for the army was far stiffer. I'd developed a casting stroke as short as it was, which was all that would work with it on tiny streams, making short casts. I transferred the old, abrupt stroke to the new Orvis. The stroke was too wristy to have enough strength to work well on long casts. It handicaps me to this day on big water. But on small streams, with just a little line out, it kept me out of trouble with brush and branches behind me and helped me get my fly onto the water in front of me.

I'm not recommending that brutal casting stroke, or such a short and stiff rod, for you. But some drift in the direction toward them might be beneficial if your current casting stroke is phlegmatic and your favorite rod flexes all the way down to its grip.

That Orvis fiberglass rod was fine for five years, until I thought I replaced it with a Leonard Duracane bamboo rod, $7^1/_2$ feet long, balanced to a 5-weight line. I turned out to be wrong.

The Leonard was fine for the majority of the fishing I was branching out to by then: matching hatches on medium and sometimes large trout streams, with the long leaders I'd once tried to apply on my cramped waters, and with flies that averaged at the tiny end of the spectrum. When I took the Leonard to my favorite small waters, proud at last to be fishing fine bamboo on waters where I'd started out fishing broken bamboo, I discovered that the rod was too slow to keep me out of trouble. My line loops were not as tight as I liked them. The rod didn't load well with just a few feet of line out, even when I used leaders its length and no longer.

That bamboo rod was sweet. But it did not suit the small streams I preferred to fish or did not suit the way I fished them. I went back to the brisk little Orvis.

I'd never met Skip Morris, who has since become so famous for his fly-fishing writing, and also a good friend, before I wrote an obscure little book of essays, *An Angler's Astoria,* in the early 1980s. Most of the book was about fishing small streams, because that is most of what I'd done in my fly-fishing life. In one chapter I described what I'd arrived at as the perfect small-stream fly rod—in theory, because I didn't own it. It would be 7 feet long, balanced to a 4-weight, double-taper line, light and crisp and bossy. Skip was a custom rod builder before he became a writer. I got a letter from him introducing himself, saying he'd read my book and would like to build that rod for me.

I was flattered. It was easy to agree.

We both thought the rod should be built in fiberglass, those times being on the border between glass and graphite. But early tries in glass failed to produce the crispness I wanted, so Skip made up a blank in graphite, taped a try-rod handle to it, and we cast it in a supermarket parking lot. It was nearly perfect. I asked for a bit more stiffness in the butt, Skip re-formed the blank to provide it, and we cast it again. We were down on our knees in that parking lot, casting at tires on parked cars, discarded lids of soda containers, anything in range.

Folks came by and asked, "Are you catching any?" You've had that happen. Skip and I were too focused to answer.

The little rod carried the line out to about sixty-five feet before it crumpled under the weight. But that was far longer than I ever planned to cast with it. I was more interested in what it did at ten to thirty feet: the more critical small-stream fly-fishing ranges that are usually ignored when a rod is tried out in a parking lot. Don't make that mistake. It's a lot easier to find a rod that is correctly loaded and accurate at fifty and even sixty feet than it is to find one that loads and places a fly where you want it at fifteen feet. Skip's did.

It was exactly what I'd always wanted: long enough at 7 feet to carry a line loop well above my head but short enough to keep it beneath the trees. It had a slight amount of stiffness taken off the tip, just enough to make it load well on a cast with only a few feet of line out. It was firm enough in the butt to keep the line loop tight and to propel the line and fly to quite some distance if needed.

The rod was the kind you get when you let an artist patiently fine-tune a perfection you can feel but are unable to describe.

That rod became my small-stream companion for a decade, all through the 1980s and into the early '90s. Those were my early writing years. Editors were not exactly clamoring for my articles, and I had lots of time to fish. I put more stream miles on Skip's rod, in more wide-spread places, than I have on any other. I never did break it, a measure of how dear I held and still hold it. I still fish it about half of my days out on small streams.

Dean Jones, a bamboo rod maker who inherited the planing forms and knowledge of five-strip builder Frank Wire, brought a rod to a workshop on aquatic insect hatches that Rick Hafele and I taught together. I cast the rod in another parking lot during a break and liked it. It was 7 feet, 4-weight, in dark cane. It was light and crisp and bossy, a lot like the Skip Morris graphite. But Dean's rod felt best to me with at least thirty feet of line out and was a bit squirrely, as far as control aiming at tires and drinking cup lids went, at distances shorter than that.

Dean and I got into a philosophical discussion about small-stream rods. I mentioned, in what I thought was passing, that I'd always wanted a bamboo rod that would show up in fishing photos on small streams. I was still trying to do more magazine writing back then. Every article required photos. The small-stream environment is deep in shadows and loaded with contrast between light and dark when the sun shines.

"If you take a picture of somebody playing a trout with a graphite rod on a forested stream," I told Dean, "the rod disappears into the background. The photo looks like some fool standing knee-deep in water, giving benedictions to a fish jumping around in front of him for some unrelated reason."

A few months after that workshop, Dean called, said he had a fly rod he wanted me to look at. I was busy, still lived in Astoria, while he lived in Portland, and I put him off. I didn't want to drive that far just to look at a fly rod. I'd seen lots. I was bad about it.

Several weeks later Dean showed up at a conclave at which I was a minor speaker. After I finished, he came up with a metal rod tube in his hands and said, "Dave, I've got that rod I want you to look at."

I uncased it. It was blonde bamboo, five-strip, gorgeous, had my name on it. I felt small enough to slip easily into its tube.

Its action duplicated the rod I'd cast in the parking lot. The first time I fished it was on a float trip down the broad Deschutes River with big and brushy stonefly drys, in a wind that howled. First impressions count for a lot, and Dean's rod got an instant bad rap. I set it aside for a season and continued to fish small streams with Skip Morris's little graphite rod.

Finally I took Dean's rod out onto a lawn and tried it with a double-taper 4-weight, then with a 5-weight. It became perfect, for me, with the heavier line, though Dean and Rick Hafele and several other friends I've asked to cast it all prefer it with the 4-weight. I think that's because I cast it most often either off my knees or at least bent low, when crouched so close to holding water that I've got to use that wristy flick-flick of a casting stroke to get the fly to where I want it on the small streams where I use it. The 5-weight loads it best for me on those short casts.

Dean's rod has become my favorite small-stream fly rod, in some small part because it brings me back to bamboo, but in largest part because, like Skip's, I use it so often that it has become a part of me. It handles so well, and with so little thought about what I am doing to make a cast happen, that my flies go where I want them almost as if I willed it.

Skip's graphite and Dean's bamboo rod have almost identical actions. Both roll-cast very well, always a necessity in a rod designed to fish small waters. Soft rods tend to roll out big hoops of line, get you in trouble with anything hanging overhead, and don't turn the leader and fly over with enough authority. A brisker rod lets you send a small hoop rolling quickly down the line. It arrives with substantial force, turns the leader over, and delivers the fly as well as an aerial cast might. That kind of roll cast gets you into far fewer troubles, is more accurate than a lazy one, and lets you land far more trout in the cramped environment of a small stream.

I've used quite a few other rods on my way to Skip's and Dean's, the two that I consider perfect. Some are just as good. One I fished only briefly, a Granger 7-foot, 4-weight that I acquired in a trade while I supported my writing by working in a sporting-goods store owned by my oldest brother. I'd just bought the Leonard and had not yet used it enough to know it wasn't right for the small-stream fishing I spent most of my time doing. I decided nobody could cast two bamboo fly rods at the same time and foolishly gave the Granger to Rick Hafele for a graduation present when he earned his master's degree in aquatic entomology. I've tried to get Rick to give it back. He isn't as foolish as I am. He does let me fish it once a season, on the small stream where he did his master's research. He goes along, keeps a close eye on me, makes me think I'm a danger to that wonderful little rod.

Rick fishes the Granger with a 4-weight, double-taper line. I prefer it with a 5-weight.

I fished one of my favorite Cascade Mountain streams with one of my favorite characters, Robert Gorman, owner of Green Mountain Rods. He let me use his 7-foot, 3-weight graphite. I loved it. After he flew home to Vermont, the same rod arrived back in the mail. Now I use it a lot, most often for presentation fishing, most often on small spring creeks.

Masako and I fished with Etsuo Kikuchi on a scattering of small streams in Hokkaido, Japan. One was brawling and of the mountain variety. Others were pastoral, with many of their features and holding lies created of concrete works designed to slow and control flows during spates. Kikuchi-san, in his fifties, sleepy-eyed, nonchalant about his casting, is the best fisherman I've ever watched work small water. He is a fan of Bjarne Fries, a six-strip bamboo rod builder from Denmark. I fished a 7-foot, 3-inch, 5-weight, was impressed immensely by the control I had with it. The same rod arrived as a wedding present when Masako and I got married. It gets fished often, but I have trouble getting it away from Masako.

In looking back over my own history with small-stream fly rods, it becomes clear to me that at each stage, the best rod I've ever owned has always been the one I've used so long that it becomes one with my hand and eye and brain. Some of them, like the broken fiberglass rod that I inherited from a deceased uncle and fished without its midsection, have been more like clubs with which to beat trout over the head than delicate casting tools to set flies softly onto small pools. But even that bad rod became a favorite after I'd used it for a couple of seasons, simply because I learned to use it, and finally to like it.

It's possible that I like the small-stream environment so much that I just grow to love whatever rod delivers me out there to fish them. I suspect I'd be happy fishing a small stream with a willow switch. But I'd not be nearly as much danger to trout as I am with one of my favorite fly rods.

My admonition to you is to use the rod you've got, then decide, while you're out on small streams, what rod you think might serve you better. The rod best for you might be far different from the rods that are most satisfying to me. Your best small-stream rod might be the one you already own and know so well.

CHAPTER FIVE

The Learning Curve

SMALL-STREAM TROUT CAN BE EASY. THEY SEE FEW FLIES BECAUSE their waters don't get much angling attention, so they get little formal education. A wide variety of food forms either emerge from the water or drop to it during an average day, so small-stream trout have rare reason to become selective, though they become as fussy as any other fish when given good reason.

Most small-stream trout are hungry most of the time, especially those in mountain and foothill headwaters. Their environments, swept clean of debris, are not as rich as those lower in river systems, where more nutrients are delivered and those that arrive are allowed to settle in. So small-stream trout are often in a rush to beat their brethren to whatever item appears on or in the water and looks like it might be food.

If you read a piece of small water carefully, puzzle out its most productive lie, and place your first cast right there, you're very likely to hook the biggest trout in whatever sort of pool it might be. That trout will have bullied its way into the best place from which to be first to food.

Small-stream trout can also be difficult. Your favorite fly, dependable though it has always been, might not remind them of anything they've eaten recently, so they fail to recognize it as edible. More often, because the small-stream environment is so constricted and the best lies are often defended by brush or other obstacles, your fly will be fine but you'll have trouble getting it onto potential holding water in a way that makes it look alive. That act requires casting control.

Control of the cast is the most critical single skill in learning to fly-fish small streams.

Because small-stream trout can be easy, once roughly the right fly is set onto approximately the right water, it takes very little time or practice to acquire enough casting skills to extract at least a few trout from easy places, which fortunately abound in most small streams. That's what gets you out there fishing them, happy to hold some trout in your hands, even if you are just getting going in fly fishing. You get rewarded by catching trout. But many of the best small-stream pools are difficult. It can take years to learn to fish all of their water with any hope of success. Even after many years, and some excellent success, when you think you've got it, you get surprised.

I had a summer assignment from *Field & Stream,* some years ago, to fish the Green River in Utah below Flaming Gorge Dam and write a piece about it. That was fun, but I had to get there. I flew into Salt Lake City, rented a car, and drove east along the skirt of the Uinta Mountains. About lunchtime, driving through a pine forest, I crossed a bridge and got a glance at what looked like a nice little trout stream bounding beneath it. I turned around, found a place to park, and had a more detailed gander at it.

The stream was so small it was not named on the bridge across it and did not show on the state map that came with the car. But its boulder-bound pools looked big enough to hold trout. I'd already bought a fishing license. I had all my gear in the trunk, including the little Skip Morris 7-foot, 4-weight and Sidekick belt bag, both of which went wherever I did in those days. I laced up felt brogues, strung my rod, tied on a size 14 Royal Wulff, grabbed the belt bag and some sort of lunch. Then I bolted downstream through the open forest, parallel to the stream, for a few hundred yards.

Squirrels scattered. A grouse exploded out. I heard a mule deer snort and thump away but didn't see it. I was too focused on the watercourse alongside me, looking for a hole in the thick brush where I could penetrate to the stream. I didn't have much time. This was a sidetrack to my mission, but I rarely have the discipline to pass up a small stream on my way to fish a big one, so I'm used to getting constantly tugged off course.

I found a gap in the crowded bitterbrush and creek dogwood, pointed my rod back behind me, bent over, and bulled through. When I straightened up, brushed all the twigs and leaves off my shoulders, and looked around, it was easy to see that I'd bumped against a different problem than I found on my home streams in the rainforests of Oregon. This was a mountain stream, steep and bouldered, obviously subject to spring spates from snowmelt. But high water had not graded the banks or driven the brush back. Instead, it had dug the channel deeper among those big boulders. That caused the formation of a series of dark and beautiful stairstep pools, all crowded in by tangles of overhanging limbs.

This is a very common type of small stream in the Rockies and in any other mountains where the stream structure is formed from hard granite rather than soft sedimentary stone. High flows are held in by hard banks. Erosional forces are concentrated on the construction of pretty pools. Brush crowds in. These pools can be very difficult to fish.

While I sat on a flat boulder munching lunch alongside that nameless Utah stream, I pondered how it might be possible to get my fly onto the pool in front of me. The pool was not long, just fifteen feet from where I sat at its foot to where I expected the best trout to be located at its head. It was narrow, almost a slot, three to at most four feet wide. The water next to the boulder on which I sat gathered and rushed into the plunge to the next pool down. I could not lay a bunch of line loosely on that fast water, under the rod tip, and use a roll cast to deliver it up to the head of the pool. The current would whisk it away before I could launch a cast.

I finished lunch without any clear idea about what I should do next to get that Royal Wulff onto water, where it might interest a trout. I stood up on the rock and looked back at the brush behind me; I thought I saw a sufficient break right in the center of it, above the slice of the stream rushing down the mountain, to thread a backcast. I lost the first fly to a branch back there.

While tying on another Royal Wulff, I gave some silent thought to the recommendation of many experts to use long rods, not short ones, on small streams. It's an idea I've never given much consideration except on small spring creeks. The theory is that you creep along the edges, stay back out of sight in the brush, and dap your fly to the water.

Three things, not counting the impracticality of thrashing through brush with a long fly rod in my hand, held me back from applying that theory on the brush-choked stream I was busy trying to figure out how to fish. First, I've always felt that the act of casting defined fly fishing, and though I don't feel it necessary to stick to that definition if I can find no way to catch trout by casting, I do enjoy fly-fishing more when I feel that I'm fly-fishing. Second, there was no way to sneak to the head of that hemmed-in pool without wading right up it, thereby frightening every trout in it. Finally, I held a short rod in my hands and was not about to trot back to the car to exchange it for a long one.

My hand and eye, suddenly and without regard to my failed brain, created a cast and shot it up there. I'll describe it as if I knew what I was doing, which I didn't. I imagined the fly sitting on the water, up there at the head of the pool where I wanted it. I stripped a scant few feet of line past the rod tip, wobbled the rod back and forth straight in front of me so briskly that the line and leader elevated off the fast water, while I held the fly by the hook bend in my off hand. Then I took aim at the head of the pool, snapped the rod into a tight roll, and let go of the fly at the same time. It was sort of a flicked forecast without any preparatory backcast.

The line jumped out, straightened in the air, and placed the fly right where my eye had imagined it. It sat for a second where bubbles arose from the little waterfall that plunked in to form the pool. Then a trout speared up and took it with a smack. I danced around on top of that boulder while the trout leaped around all over that pool.

It was a wild cutthroat, prettily spotted and painted with some blush colors not found on the ones I'd ever caught at home. It was fifteen inches long and fairly hefty. That was oversize for the size pool from which it arose, according to any calculations I'd learned to make about the size of small-stream trout. This spoke well of all the provender that must fall from the shrubbery crowding the creek.

I released the trout, fished back up to the bridge, and caught about the same number of trout from the bouldered pools as I lost flies to the encroaching scenery. In a small but satisfying number of pools, I was able to present my dry fly with the normal sequence of backcast and forecast, and thereby catch trout. In others, I was able to use a roll cast to fish a pool. But in most places, that strange cast spontaneously created by my hand and eye, without instruction from the conscious part of my brain, solved the situation.

That was all. I broke down my rod, changed out of my wet brogues, got back into the car, and hurried on toward the Green River. But I had a head start on a happy trip before I got there.

All common casts and creative casts, whether for small-stream pools or for presentation fishing over the trickiest rising trout on spring creek and tailwater flats, are built on the basic casting stroke, consisting of backcasts and forecasts. You need to learn the basic cast first, and if you've already learned it, you need to execute it often enough to make it something your hand and eye can perform without any direction from the thinking part of your brain. You need to repeat it often enough to commit it to what is called *kinetic memory,* which is a fancy way of saying that the basic cast becomes automatic.

Often I hear the admonishment to learn this by practicing daily on a lawn or in a park. That's fine, and perhaps best for getting started. Practice separated from fishing will never hurt your casting stroke and will in the end help it a lot because the more you do it the more it becomes something you can do without thinking. But my recommendation is to get as much practice as possible while out fishing.

I also recommend that you do as much casting as you can, whether it's over small water or green grass, with the same rod. Don't switch around, beyond what it takes to determine the one right rod for you, and the right line for the rod, because each rod responds differently to the pressures applied to it. The more you learn about what your favorite rod will do, the better you'll be able to cast in tight situations. And you'll be able to do that casting without any conscious thought about it.

Though it could be described in more complicated terms, the basic casting stroke at its core is a repeated four-part movement: *load* and *power* the backcast, *load* and *power* the forecast. The loading movement in both directions takes slack out of the line and places the rod tip in position to transfer whatever force is applied to the rod directly to the line. In essence, loading tightens the line against the tip and gets a bend going in the rod that will be deepened and released by the power part of the stroke.

The power movement drives the rod, whether forward or back, briskly and with considerable force. The bent rod unbends and unleashes its force. The line accepts this force from the tip and is accelerated into considerable speed. The line loops over the rod tip and unfurls in the air. The shorter the power stroke, the closer the top of your loop will be to its bottom, hence the tighter your loop and the less space it will occupy in the air. The longer the power stroke, the farther the upper part of the loop will be from the bottom, and the more open the loop and the more space it will take up as it unfurls. That is why a short and sharp stroke, with a stop at its end that is almost a bump, works well on small streams, where you'll usually be casting in confined quarters with little line out. A short power stroke ended by a sudden stop builds line speed abruptly and tosses the line out in a very tight loop.

The tighter your casting loop, the less trouble it will deliver you into. The more open and lazy the loop, the more it's likely to encounter brush behind and branches above. So, as you tighten up almost everything about the way you approach small waters—the length of your rod and the leader attached to your line and the distance between your casting position and the water you desire to fish—on account of the restrictions of the environment, you also tighten up the length of your power stroke in order to tidy up the shape of your casting loop.

As you increase your experience with the basic cast and perform sufficient repetitions, you'll begin to feel the line telling you what to do with the rod in order to make the kind of cast you're after happen. A fly line has weight. The sense of this weight, when applied against the rod tip, will be transferred through the sensitive rod to your hand on the grip and will tell you when to apply the next part of the cast, whether it's load or power, forward or back. If it's the power part of the stroke, the weight of the line against the rod will tell you how much force to put into the stroke to get the fly to where you want it.

There's no way in the world that I can tell you how all this feels. If you cast enough, you'll learn to feel the line speaking to you through the rod, telling you what to do with the rod to make the right things happen.

This feel is the reason you choose a rod that is somewhat brisk—and to be brisk, it must be somewhat stiff in its middle parts and down into its butt—but has a sensitive tip. Feel is also the reason I recommend you consider choosing a line that other folks, especially rod manufacturers, might consider one weight heavy for the rod. If you're making short casts and the line is light, it's much more difficult to feel the weight of the line plying back and forth in the air, exerted against the tip of the rod, telling you what to do.

Your casting, even with a short power stroke, will still be extremely graceful when done right. It will receive that grace from your fine feel for the loading part of the stroke. As the line unfurls either in front of you or behind you, you'll sense when it begins to straighten and it's time to bring your rod forward to load the line against the tip. When your timing gets good, you'll bring the rod forward in the load at precisely the moment the line is straight but before it begins to drop. That kind of casting is pretty to watch.

If there is any advantage to casting on lawns, beyond necessary repetitions, it is being able to turn and watch your line loop unfurl on the backcast. Watching for that right moment when the line is straight but not beginning to drop, and beginning the loading movement then, lets you load the rod with maximum line weight against it. When the rod is brought forward with all the line weighted against it, you get the best feel for it and can respond to it with just the right amount of force applied in just the right direction. The loading movement becomes slow and deliberate, even delicate, followed by that abrupt power stroke that drives the line quickly forward, or back in the backcast. The sweeping loading movement and the patient unfurling of the loop in the air make the cast grace itself.

Once you've got the basic cast down, then it's time to add some variations that solve specific small-stream situations. Most can be viewed as ways to avoid obstacles that infringe on the backcast or forecast area and, therefore, make it difficult to get your fly onto the water with the basic cast.

You can view these casts as separate from the basic cast and practice each before attempting to apply it against trout. I recommend you do that, but advise it a bit feebly. It won't hurt to have the motions of the different casts down before you try to use them to draw trout up. But you should also consider them as modifications you work on the basic cast that you already know, in order to keep your fly out of some trouble you recognize when you creep into position to make a cast to water you think should provide you a trout. In that sense, they'll serve you best when you learn to apply them on water in response to specific problems.

The first variant of the basic cast is the sidearm cast. This is nothing more than the basic cast flopped over ninety degrees, onto its side. The rod is held straight out from you at somewhere around shoulder height. Of course, you'll often do it off your knees, when fishing, or while bent over, lowering your shoulder nearer to the ground. Backcasts and forecasts are made with the rod parallel to the ground, alongside your shoulder, rather than perpendicular, straight up over your shoulder. Line loops, in the sidearm cast, unfurl back and forth somewhat short of your own height above the ground.

The sidearm cast lowers the line ten feet or more, as opposed to the standard cast. If the problem you're trying to solve is tree limbs overhead, then lowering the travel of the looping line is a terrific advantage. Because water tends to clear a path for itself, it's very common to find pools where, by crouching or kneeling and keeping your cast tilted off to the side, you can sail your backcast low over the water downstream from you, then shoot your forecast out low and onto the water you want to fish upstream from you.

On typical freestone streams, most of them in the foothills, many of them the average small-stream water type that most of us fish most of the time, some ability to tilt your rod into a sidearm cast will be helpful on about half of the pools you fish during an average day. That's a lot of casts and can add up to a lot of extra trout.

You will cast enough, if you fish small streams often enough, to begin to feel the line telling you what to do with the rod. The sidearm cast can help you reach this level more quickly, because the line loops are laid out alongside you, where you can watch them unfold. A friend of mine who guides often has to teach his clients fly casting before he can get them into fish. When a client has trouble, my friend often recommends tipping the rod over into a sidearm cast, then watching the way each cast unfolds fore and back. It's an excellent way to spot troubles with your own casting stroke.

It's also an excellent way to learn what the line is telling you about what to do with the rod, and when, to get the response you'd like in a cast. When you are able to get down on one knee and cast with your rod straight out from your upraised knee, and keep your casting plane about that same height above the water or above a gravel bar behind you, without letting the line touch down and therefore interfere with your intentions, you'll be able to extract trout from some pretty difficult situations.

My home streams, because of their sedimentary landscapes and winter spates, have lots of clean gravel bars overhung by low branches. I've learned to fish them with a sidearm cast that scorches the earth. I won't detail for you the frustration I went through before I learned to keep my casts above those stones but beneath those branches *most of the time,* because I'm not sure you'd like to hear the language involved. That was a major part of my own long learning curve on small streams, which remains exactly as far from ended as yours: We'll both be learning about small-stream fishing the rest of our lives.

After you've learned to tilt your cast off to the side, it's critical to learn to tilt the casting plane in another direction. On many small streams, especially but far from exclusively those of the meadow variety, the problem is tall grass and shrubbery growing from the ground up into your backcast area rather than limbs draping into it from above. I've mentioned the many clean gravel bars of my favorite forested streams. I've failed to mention that as summer heats up, foxglove and mullein stems begin to tower along them. By August these plants are at head height. Where no trees drop branches down to overhang them, the problem to solve is lofting a backcast above them.

The solution looks easy at first sight: Just stand up, keep the rod high, and my own height plus the length of my rod will keep the backcast out of danger. It's not a problem. The problem then is that I'm standing there waving a stick around, in sight of any trout around. That will work to get the cast out there. It won't work to catch many trout. But don't discount it as a solution. If the water you're about to fish is a frothed current tongue or plunge-pool pocket, broken enough on the surface to keep trout from spotting you out of their lies along the bottom, then stand up, haul off, and cast. They won't see you, and you will catch them.

If you need to kneel, or if you can stand but the obstacles behind you are higher than normal backcast height, then you need to tilt your casting plane down in front and up behind. In the basic cast, done while standing and with no tilt of the casting plane, the fly line moves through backcast and forecast at about the height of, and parallel to, the eaves of a house. The key is that the forecast and backcast both travel at the same height above the ground. The fly line draws an approximately straight ruler line from the backcast through the rod tip into the forecast. If your backcast and forecast fail to travel in the same plane, you're courting troubles of one sort or another, mostly tailing loops. These happen when the upper part of your loop dips beneath the lower part of the loop. The fly catches the line and your cast ends in a mess. That happens a lot when you break the plane of the cast.

The casting plane of a basic cast can be tipped in any direction a fishing situation might call for, without incurring any problems in the cast. It's difficult to imagine a situation in which you would want to drop your backcast low and send your forecast high, at least on a small stream. If you're casting for distance where there are no obstacles behind you and the wind is at your back, tilting your backcast down toward the ground and your forecast up into the air lets you send your line high so it can catch the wind and fly farther. That's not a small-stream situation.

It's common on small streams to find pools that can be fished best by tipping the casting plane down in front, up over obstacles behind. It works when I'm kneeling in front of those foxglove and mullein stems. The cast is easy to execute. Just aim the forecast at a point low over the water in front, the backcast high over the problem behind. The straight line of the casting plane is maintained; it is just no longer parallel with the water, the ground, or the eaves of a house.

A cast with a tilted plane is limited by how far in front you can extend the forecast without having it smack into the water, which would frighten trout, which brings up the bit of advice to keep your measuring forecasts off to the side of the water you intend to fish, if it's an option. If you make a couple of forecasts low over the lie on which you intend to place your fly, to measure the right amount of line out, there is some chance that trout in the lie will have either fled or pulled the covers over their heads by the time your fly gets onto the water. Trout are wary about predation from overhead and don't like anything moving around up there.

They also don't like anything smacking into the water near them, which is why the distance you can cast by tilting the plane of the forecast down is limited. If you're kneeling, you'll be able to cover just about twenty feet of water. If you're standing, you can tilt the plane and reach out to thirty-five or forty feet, enough to cover all but the biggest of small-stream pools.

The sidearm cast and tilted plane, between them, go a long way toward solving the largest of small-stream problems: obstacles anywhere in your backcast area. The first thing to do, when you approach any pool, is to read its water, scout out the likely lies of trout. Move into the best position to fish the closest of these lies. Figure out where you'd like your fly to land. Then observe front and back for any obstacles to the path your line must take in the air to place your fly in that particular spot.

Look for a clear area into which you can insert your backcast. At rare times, nothing will be back there within range, and you can ignore that half of the casting problem. More often there will be things to avoid, but some minor adjustment, say dropping your cast slightly sidearm or tilting the casting plane up a bit in back, will solve it.

Sometimes things get crowded back there, and you're forced to look for smaller areas of clearance.

With an accumulation of experience, your subconscious will begin to make most of these calculations for you, and it will make them correctly most of the time. As you fish more and cast constantly, your hand and eye, directed by the part of your brain that you're not aware is working for you, will find the opening in the backcast area, place your cast into and out of it, without asking you to think about it. But that won't happen if you have not paused and taken time to run your eyes over the area.

If you don't look all around you before you cast, you're more than likely to get hung up on something you've not noticed. Sometimes the only hole that will allow a backcast in a crowded background is so small that the best way to hit it is to turn to face it, aim your forecast into it, and make your backcast the delivery stroke. This decreases the chance that you'll get hung up, up there, but also decreases the chance that your fly will land precisely where you'd like it, out where trout hang out. It will let you fish some bits of water that you'd otherwise need to pass up.

It's often helpful to position your feet—your knees, if you're on them—so that you can turn to follow and observe both your backcasts and forecasts. That entails facing halfway away from the water you want to fish. It gives you a great advantage in tight situations, which are the most common kinds on small streams. Take advantage of whatever footwork, handwork, and eyework you can to make your fishing less frustrating and more productive.

The steeple cast, which sends the backcast towering high overhead, can help you avoid obstacles such as shrubbery at the banks of a meadow stream that grows so tall behind you that you cannot get above it by merely tilting the casting plane. To execute the steeple cast, turn halfway into the backcast and aim it high over whatever is back there, or precisely into some hole in whatever foliage is up there. As the loop of the backcast unfurls, turn to the front and aim your forecast straight toward where you want it to go.

The steeple cast breaks the plane of the cast, lifting the backcast high but sending the forecast at rod tip height. If you were to diagram it, the forecast and backcast would form an open and tipped V, with the point of the V located at your rod tip. When you break the casting plane in this way, you get into frequent problems with tailing loops. They come with the territory. If you cannot get your fly onto the water in any other way, use the steeple cast and put up with the occasional collapse of your cast.

In truth, I fish small streams constantly but use the steeple cast rarely. It solves one problem but causes another. It's best to solve the same problem by shifting your casting position, if possible, in a way that lets you use a sidearm cast or tilt the plane of your cast without breaking it.

Many situations that seem best solved by the steeple cast are actually perfect for the roll cast. You've got a tall wall of brush, wheat grasses, mullein stems, or even a hedgerow right behind you. The water is open in front of you, or possibly overhung by limbs. A sidearm cast, tilted plane, and even steeple cast would crash right into the background. In such circumstances, where there is no way to make a backcast, you can still place a fly easily and accurately out to twenty and thirty feet, and with some accuracy out to forty feet and farther, with a roll cast. But you can't do it with a noodle of a rod, another reason to use one that is at least moderately stiff for small-stream fishing. You'll resort to the roll cast a lot on a day spent fishing an average small stream.

The roll cast, appearances to the contrary, is a modification of the basic cast. I emphasize that because most folks think the term *roll* refers to the stroke used to make the cast. It actually refers to the hoop that is driven down the line. You load the rod by drawing the line toward you on the water. You drive that hoop with a standard power stroke, aimed straight at where you want the fly to land. If you try to drive the hoop with a rolling motion of the rod tip, you'll send an open, feeble circle flopping along the line. The fly might jump into the air and end up landing not far from your feet.

A proper roll cast begins with some line out on the water. This can be stripped from the reel, pulled out beyond the rod tip, and piled onto the water in front of your feet. If that near water is flowing so fast that the line is swept downstream, then you must shift position until you've got modestly still water under your rod tip. A roll cast is best done from off to the calm side of a pool, rather than right in the gathering water of its tailout.

Once you've got the right amount of line on the water, then you enter the loading part of the cast. The roll cast depends on the tension of the water's surface to load the rod. It's not a cast you can practice on a lawn.

The rod is loaded by tilting the tip back behind your shoulder at about a forty-five-degree angle. That movement will start the line on the water sliding in toward the rod tip, now behind you. Watch the length of line between the rod tip and the point where the line first lies on the water. When this short length of line between the rod tip and the water travels behind the rod and sags into a bow, drive the rod forward with a crisp, short power stroke. The shorter this power stroke, the smaller and faster the hoop that will travel down the line. The slower and therefore longer the power stroke, the more open and lazy the hoop that will amble down the line.

The hoop should travel through the air, not on the water. It should lift the leader and fly into the air and turn them over above the water, then set them onto it somewhat straight, not all in a pile. The smaller the hoop, the lower you can drive it and the tighter the spot into which you can deliver your fly, especially if you're dealing with branches overhanging the water you want to fish. That's why you practice the roll cast until you can control the size of the hoop by adjusting the length and speed of the power stroke. But that, like all things applied to small-stream fishing, takes time and experience, which in this case is best acquired out on trout water, because water is required to load the cast.

Once you learn to get your fly out to a reasonable distance with the roll cast, you'll open up lots of places you were previously unable to fish. It's especially valuable on small streams for a couple of reasons, one obvious, the other less so. The roll cast works well on small streams because of the number of pools where a backcast is blocked by brush. That's obvious. It's a tight environment, perfect for the roll cast. But the roll cast also works on small streams because, by their stairstep nature, they tend toward short pools with central current tongues and slower water off to the sides. On the average small-stream pool, you can take a position at the edge of the pool, with brush and trees behind you, strip out line and lay it onto slower water beneath the rod tip, then roll it out to faster water.

That's not always true on larger streams and rivers, where you tend to fish a broad sheet of water all flowing at a relatively even speed. It's difficult to use a roll cast when you're standing at the edge of a big riffle, backed up against trees, trying to roll your fly from one bit of fast water out to a different bit of the same swift riffle.

Where the water is not shaped right for a roll cast, which usually means you can't lay the line on moving water at your feet and have it stay there, you might be able to employ what I've come to call the *punch cast*. It's the one that first came to me on that small Uinta Mountain stream where deer and grouse and trout were flying all around. I should probably call it the dance cast, because the idea is to get a bunch of line dancing in the air under the rod tip, then flick it out. But I call it the punch cast because that's what the power stroke that makes it go looks like: a short punch thrown at somebody's chin. Maybe that's a bad metaphor for a fly-fishing cast, but follow along; we'll just be giving that chin a tap.

As with many of the casts that work well on small streams, this one is too wristy to involve fatal force. What I mean by wristy is this: The rod is loaded by getting the line tugging against the rod tip in the air, then the power stroke is made by driving your forearm forward a very short way, and at the same time driving your wrist forward in a motion that is no more than a flick. That is all wrong for the casting school approach, which is designed for distance. In the school-approved power stroke, the wrist is held rigid. All power comes from driving the forearm forward.

That makes sense for distance; the forearm is a lot more powerful than the wrist. Imagine that chin again; put it on somebody you don't like. Cock your fist a foot from it, stiffen your wrist, and drive a punch forward. That will hurt. Now hold your fist about two inches from the chin, cock your wrist, and hit it again, using mostly your wrist. It's just a tap.

That tap has little force behind it. The same movement made with a fly rod in your hand won't accelerate a long, loaded fly line and throw it through the air with much speed, which is why it's a poor way to cast a fly if you're casting for distance. But that quick, wristy stroke can take a short line that's already loaded against the rod tip and power it abruptly into a tight loop heading right toward where you want it, which on a small stream should not be very far away.

This power stroke should not be fueled fully from the wrist. As the wrist turns over, the forearm drives forward scant inches at the same time. You might say—this is really stretching the analysis of a movement that happens so abruptly it's hard to parse any of it out—that the forearm provides most of the power and the flick of the wrist installs most of the speed.

However you describe it, it amounts to a short, quick flick: an unpowerful punch that you won't find useful in a fight, that will be a handicap if you carry it over into the kinds of fly fishing that require long casts, but one that you'll find useful in your small-stream fishing.

Once you've danced that line in the air, punch it out. If circumstances are so tight that it's dangerous even to let the fly dance back and forth in front of you, hold it by the hook bend with your off hand. Get the line dancing until you can feel it trying to tug the fly out of your grip. Then punch it out and let go of the fly just as the outgoing line comes tight against. This will let you get one good cast onto water that is surrounded by encroaching limbs. On that kind of water you're very likely to catch a fish on that first cast, because most fishermen take a mournful look at such a difficult place and pass by it.

A punch cast takes some time to set up—gathering in the line and getting ahold of the fly—so you're not very likely to want more than that first good cast on the average pool so tightly constricted. On many hemmed pools, however, that one cast can serve to get your line and fly out to where you can return the fly to the potential holding water time and again with miniaturized roll casts: rolls made with the line short, the rod held low and tucked in against your body, the power stroke brief and probably weak because if you make a strong move in such tight surroundings, you're liable to whack your rod tip against something and break it.

If all this sounds esoteric and difficult, that's because it is until you begin to feel the line telling you what to do with the rod. After that you'll discover some creative casts of your own that solve situations you encounter in your travels up and down your own small streams.

The learning curve on small waters is long and can be loaded with frustration if you try to push yourself too fast. If you take time to observe the obstacles in all directions, whenever you approach a new piece of water, and figure out the best position from which to fish it and the best cast with which to fish it, you'll reduce your problems and increase your catch. When you begin *feeling* solutions to situations rather than thinking them and begin creating casts to solve them, you'll have reached the point in the learning curve where you're one with small streams, and you might even find you prefer them to big ones.

CHAPTER SIX

Reading Small Pools

ENERGY FROM SUNLIGHT GETS CONVERTED INTO FUEL BY PHOTOSYN-
thesis, both on the streambottom by algae and in streamside vegetation
by leaf-bearing trees. Aquatic insects browse on both the thin layer of
algae that grows on bottom rocks and on leaves that fall to the water.
These insects are the primary aquatic converters of plant material to
animal life.

Trout eat the insects that turn plant material into animate life. In
that way small-stream trout become bright, eager, and active condensations of sunlight itself. These bits of brightness that we call trout have
needs they must satisfy in order to survive. We use those needs against
them to find and catch them.

Trout hold where they do in moving water according to the way it
provides shelter from forceful currents, offers protection from overhead
predation, and furnishes food to eat. Trout have other needs as well—
for example, for water that is cool enough and holds enough oxygen for
them to survive, and for gravel beds clean enough that they can spawn
successfully, thereby sowing the seeds for the next small-stream trout
generation. But cool water, sufficient oxygen, and spawning gravel are
long-term needs, without the satisfaction of which there would simply
be no trout in that stream.

Day to day, small-stream trout can be found in particular lies
based on their three needs for shelter from currents, protection from

predators, and adequate provisions. When you try to figure out the most likely lies for small-stream trout, in that initial step upon arriving at a pool that we call *reading the water* to figure out where to cast flies upon it, the first things to consider are the basic needs of the trout and the way the water in that pool is shaped to meet them.

Water flowing through any small pool, whether that pool is located in a mountain, freestone, or meadow stream, enters at the head, flows through the body, and exits at the tailout of the pool. That is the essential anatomy of any trout-stream pool: head, body, and tailout.

The head might be formed by a small waterfall that plunges into it, a brisk riffle that bounds down to it, or a run that ambles in and spreads out to form it. The body of a pool might be a short to long current tongue with shallower and slower water off to the sides. It also might be a run of water, slow or fast, that flows at a relatively steady depth above submerged boulders or glancing among protruding ones. The body of what we consider a classic pool, the kind in which the current slows almost to a stop and the bottom drops away to dark depths, is common on some small streams but is far from the average type of pool you'll fish on small waters.

The tailout of a pool might be an abrupt but slight brake to fast currents just before they topple over into the next pool, or it might be an hourglass sort of narrowing, gathering, and lifting of spread currents preparatory to sliding them into the riffle or run that drops into the next pool. But all pools, even pocket-water pools that are not much more than hesitations in the general rush of frothed water, have those three parts: head, body, and tailout.

A prime trout lie is not always found in a pool, though most in small streams are. An excellent lie might be formed wherever a boulder interrupts the flow of a riffle or run or where a trench in the bottom of moderate to fast water forms a slot of deep water: a small place where trout can find shelter from fast currents, obtain protection from predators, and have food delivered to them. Wherever you find the needs of trout met, you'll find trout and have a chance to catch them, whether it's in a riffle, run, pool, or pocket.

Placing theory about reading water into action, you look at flows to assess how boulders and other bottom features interrupt currents so trout don't have to fight them. You look at depth or frothed surfaces for the way they might or might not hide trout from kingfishers and herons. You look at currents for the way they might gather and deliver the foods that trout eat. With time and experience, this assessment becomes quick, almost automatic. Like your assessment of overhanging limbs and other obstacles that might hinder a backcast, your quick read of a pool you're about to fish will, with time, be done less consciously than subconsciously. But it won't be inaccurate. That read for lies will be based on your register of experiences about what the water looked like where you cast and hooked trout in your past, and what the water looked like where you cast but hooked nothing.

You do not need to consciously notice the shape of the water where you hook every fish, nor do you need to jot down mental notes about currents and depths and obstructions in that pinpoint place. I've tried it and discovered that it's almost impossible to do. The second a trout takes my fly, I get busy dealing with setting the hook, playing the trout, bringing it to my outstretched hand. After I release it, stand up, dry my fly, and apply floatant for the next cast, I finally remember to look back to the water. By then I can never recall precisely where the fly was riding when it got whacked.

That's natural. If you have the same problem, don't worry about it. Your subconscious will sort it all out. The next time it notices water shaped that same way, a few pools up or a few days later, it will know right where to set the fly. But it takes lots of time to gather subconscious data and build that bank of information about all small-stream water types. So that's an assignment to go fishing a lot, if you need one.

While you build that data bank in your brain, it helps if you apply what you know of the needs of trout and begin to notice where the water might meet them. Your close observations of water just before you cast to it will furnish material for later processing by your subconscious. Your conscious assessment of lies will also be right so often that success will propel you along, keeping you happy while your body of experience builds.

You'll have no trouble enjoying small streams from the day you first fish them, because you'll begin at once to catch trout from them. But you'll begin to insert yourself into small streams, become one with them, when both your casting skills and ability to read water become less conscious and more subconscious.

To get to that point, you go fishing as often as life lets you, approach small-stream pools from downstream, kneel next to them, and examine them carefully before you begin to fish them. That examination itself is the first major step toward success. It took me years to slow down and begin looking around before I cast. That pause at the foot of each pool is useful for more than locating potential lies. When trout are rising sporadically to occasional insects, which is the most common kind of surface feeding in small streams, you'll never notice the rises if you rush up and cast before giving trout time to expose themselves.

The first place you look for lies, in the normal approach to a pool from downstream, is the tailout where currents gather, usually so close to you that you need to keep low so trout holding there can't spot you. When trout hold in the currents of a tailout, they will be found only in places where some structure softens the accelerating flow. They might lie along the bottom in slight trenches, or just upstream or down from small boulders.

If a trench or boulder is present in a tailout, you can be almost certain at least one trout will be located there, most likely one of the largest in the pool. A tailout lie gives a trout a look at any terrestrial insect that plops to the surface of the pool ahead of it, and a similar chance at any aquatic insect that emerges from the body of the pool and does not get eaten before it floats to the tailout. The tailout lie is excellent for a trout so long as there is some sort of satisfaction of its needs for shelter from the current and protection from predators.

Rocks and trenches might break the current, but they also must offer sufficient depth, say a foot or more, before trout will have protection from predators. The need for food, provided abundantly on many tailouts, often overrides the need for protection. Trout back down to tailouts from safer lies up in the deeper body of the pool, even at the risk of exposure to birds and beasts, if enough aquatic insects hatch or terrestrial insects fall to the pool to feed them well. When they do hold on tailouts without sufficient depth for protection from predators, small-stream trout will be extremely spooky.

If you've ever wondered what caused those almost invisible V-wakes that arrow away from tailouts when you approach small-stream pools too carelessly, now you know: They're fleeing trout. You're not going to catch them, and you're not likely to catch any others that they've frightened during that startled dash up the length of the pool you're about to fish.

If the bottom beneath a tailout is all fine pebbles or gravel, you can usually forget about finding trout there. Such small stuff does not disrupt the current sufficiently to form lies. Even if it does, trout lying over a fine gravel background will be so exposed to predators that they avoid such a lie except during a heavy hatch of aquatic insects or fall of terrestrials.

Reading the body of a pool is both more and less difficult than reading a tailout. On one hand, it is usually the larger part of the pool and might have quite a few more parts. On the opposite hand, its parts can be more easily read in terms of the way they meet the needs of trout. Most obviously, the main current is the delivery system for all the food that moves through the pool. Trout will almost always be located with some relationship to that current, in a position where they can dash into it to intercept what it trots either over them on the surface or past them submerged.

The main current tongue, whether it is central or pushed up against one of the sides, also erodes out the deepest depths in a pool. In a typical small-stream pool—one with a riffle at its head, a central current tongue that is brisk at the head and slows toward the tail, and a tailout that gathers the current and accelerates it once again—the deepest water will be somewhere under the current tongue between the head and the point where it loses most of its force.

If the pool is long and the current tongue dissipates its strength in almost still water when the stream is at fishable levels, you'll usually find the greatest depth at the lower end of the current tongue. That is where the flow attains its greatest erosional strength when the water is too high to fish, which is when most erosion happens. It shouldn't seem a secret that a prime lie in such a pool starts right where the current peters out over dark depths.

If the main current in a pool makes just a short run before dropping into whatever kind of water delivers it to the next step, the deepest slot might run the length of the pool, and trout might hold anywhere along that length. Where you find features such as trenches or boulders interrupting the current along the bottom, you'll find trout directly beneath the main current, because the depth that the current has carved offers trout the most protection from predators.

It's rare that you'll be able to read the surface of a current tongue and determine exactly where specific features might lie along the bottom beneath it. The top is usually too bouncy to let you look down through the water column, the very factor that protects trout there from birds hovering overhead. But that bounciness reports that the bottom is featured, it has potential lies all along it, and you should fish all of it.

Wherever the main current of a pool butts against a bank or cliff and is turned by it, an eddy or at least a slight backwater will form on the inside of the turn. This will usually be over deep water and is obviously a gathering spot for all sorts of food that falls to the surface of the pool or emerges out of it. It's a prime lie for a trout.

When a riffle or run drops into a pool and butts almost directly against a cliff rather than hitting it at an angle and being turned by it, an eddy lie will form on the near side, but another will also set whirling on the opposite side, across the current from your wading position. This eddy is a prime lie, but it's often a very difficult one to fish. You must cast across the main current and set your fly onto the slower current on the other side of it. That can cause drag.

The slow to almost still water along the edges of the body of a small-stream pool, whether shallow or not, can hold trout at times, but not nearly as often as that beneficial main current slot. Trout move to the slack edges if they find some sort of protection from overhead predation there and, at the same time, an abundance of food falling from overhead. Usually the same brush and branches that provide the cover also offer the food.

I've had many June days improved by the presence of green inchworms dangling from conifers and alders along shallow edges with almost imperceptible currents. One of my favorite flies is an Olive Beadhead nymph, tied slender on a size 12 to 14 hook. It's a fly of my own devising, and I'm no deviser of flies. But I was unable to find one like it, so I made it up. It was not in response to those inchworms. I tied it first to imitate green rockworms that are abundant in riffles on my favorite big river, the brawling Deschutes. But I had a few of them with me one day when inchworms were busy rappelling into the water along a favorite small stream.

I'd not noticed them until I paused to have lunch and saw a trout feeding in water where I didn't think it belonged, just inches deep and barely moving. The trout fed with vigorous swirls and seemed always to be darting forward from its lie in the shadow of a drooping hemlock bough to take something up under the bough. I couldn't see anything on the water to prompt such vigor from the trout.

My custom in such a situation is to fumble my sandwich into the water, grab my rod, shoot first, ask questions only after I fail to catch the trout. But I'd been having an unusually bad day, given the excellent conditions of sunshine and warmth that normally promise lots of trout to dry flies on that stream. So I held fire, continued to eat lunch, watched that trout awhile, and tried to figure out what it was doing. It rose two or three more times before I finally was able to see an inchworm drop slowly from the bough toward the stream until it was in it.

That was its undoing.

I looked through my single fly box, found a few of those green beadheads I'd hate to be without on any trout water. I tied one on, slip-knotted a wisp of yellow yarn to the leader three feet above the fly, and worked into a position from which I could flick that simple nymph rig just upstream from the hemlock bough. The current delivered it slowly downstream.

That was the trout's undoing.

I saw the fish shoot forward eagerly, saw the indicator take a swift dive, set the hook, and held on. The trout was twelve inches long, over-length for that tiny stream, and admirably plump.

The head of a small-stream pool, where the water rushes into it from upstream, is rarely the most productive part of the pool. I think that's because the most comfortable lies are not often right up there in the rush of things. Trout that hold a bit downstream from the head of the pool, where things have slowed down, are usually able to winnow more food from the current and lose less energy fighting it.

The exceptions are notable because they'll provide extra trout on an average day astream if you notice where the head of a pool might be productive and, therefore, take time to fish it rather than passing by it. I've already mentioned those tiny eddies of almost black water that form behind boulders at the heads of pools in mountain streams. Trout will hold there early in the season, when the water is still somewhat high and trout lies beneath the main current tongue might be a little too brisk for comfort. I've also mentioned riffle corners, where the water entering the head of a pool descends over a riffle, right into water that is deep enough to give overhead protection from predators. If every pool were shaped this way, with water at least a foot deep right at the head, every pool would provide two opportunities at nice trout, one on each side, tucked right up in the corner of every riffle. Unfortunately, the average small-stream riffle is too pushy in the main flow, and too shallow alongside it, for the happiness of trout. Recall those needs: Trout can't fight a strong current, and they don't enjoy being exposed needlessly to predation.

Trout that hang out at the edges of entering riffles, in water just inches deep, get weeded out of the gene pool quickly by kingfishers and herons on any small stream I've fished. But give that same location a foot or two of depth, a surface with a bit of bounce on top to further hide them, and a nice trout will spend time there, right in the soft spot next to the swiftness of the riffle. As you fish your way up a current tongue, take careful notice of the highest bit of water where the current tongue enters the pool. If it has a bouldered eddy at its edge or a soft spot with some depth next to a graveled riffle, set your fly there. Work it right up into the corner, and let it sit as long as you can.

Often a trout will spear up to take it. But just as often, in my experience, one won't.

If not, reel up and head up to the next pool, read its parts, and fish them according to your assessment of where they might hold trout.

CHAPTER SEVEN

Parts Between Pools

AN ABUNDANCE OF TROUT, AND MOST OF THE BIGGEST ONES, ARE found in small-stream pools. These pools form prime lies because they provide the three basic needs of trout: shelter from currents, protection from predators, and delivery of food. Pools have slower currents, deeper water, and broader surface areas to gather more food than most other parts of streams.

Many places between pools also meet the needs of trout, and wherever they do, you'll find trout holding in them. It's quite likely they'll not meet those needs as well as pools, and the trout holding in them will often be smaller, but sometimes you'll get surprises.

A mile-long stretch of one of my favorite foothill streams has an unusual structure, caused by an ancient lava flow. Its deepest pools are carved into basaltic bedrock. They're deep, they're slow, they have lots of surface area, but they're nearly barren of any but small trout. I was not able to figure out why until I took up the minor study of insects that trout eat. Then I realized that these pools have very few rocks on their bottoms and, therefore, very few niches for aquatic nymphs or larvae.

Terrestrials fall to them. Big cased caddis larvae crawl across their unfeatured bottoms. But kick-net samples turn up no mayflies or stoneflies and only scant numbers of the smaller caddis larvae that make up such a large component of most small-stream trout diets. I know small trout live in the pools and feed on the terrestrials. But I speculate those pebble-cased caddis don't dare to venture out onto the bare streambed until they've grown large enough to be safe from the size trout that survive in the pools.

It is not speculation that almost all of the gravel and cobble and boulders in the streambed have been deposited in long runs between these bedrock pools. I don't know what forces of hydraulics have cleaned out the pools almost completely and placed all life-providing rockworks in the runs. I do know that this has shifted the greatest abundance of insect niches from the pools into the runs. That's where trout find the most food, and that's where the largest trout in this stretch of the stream hang out.

For many youthful years, I fished the beautiful pools of this part of the stream diligently but plunged through the runs with no more than a few casual casts. The pools upstream and down from this section of bedrock pools held good numbers of fine trout. The runs and riffles between pools upstream and down from this stretch held few fish and, with a few exceptions that were obvious lies, deserved neglect.

It took years, during which I resented this part of one of my favorite streams because I had to wade through it without much hope of catching trout from it, before I learned that the trout were there. I just needed to fish the right water to catch them. The right water turned out to be in the runs in any pocket or trench or behind any boulder in water that was more than a foot or so deep. If trout were able to dig in, get out of the force of the flow, and hide under a rock from the kingfishers and herons that were fierce on the stream, they'd be present and easily accounted for.

They were either less well fed than trout in pools or a lot more accustomed to making quick decisions about food. A fly shown to them, whether surface or sunk, would be instantly struck by them.

As I began to fish this water between the pools more frequently and much more diligently, I discovered that it held trout on average the same size that they might have been in the pools in that stretch of stream if the pools had a normal bottom structure. I learned, in addition, that the largest of those trout could always be caught in pockets or beneath slight current tongues that were adjacent, upstream or down, to the pools where I'd at one time expected to catch them.

That proximity of large trout to pools, but not in pools, is an aspect of this stretch of stream that I learned through trial and error but am unable to explain. My only guess is that the trout view the depths of the nearby pool as a bomb shelter and stay near it so they can dive into it when they come under attack.

It's also possible that the trout roam and feed in the pools at night, then move into the nearest holding lies in the faster water to wait out the day. If that's true, though, I have no idea what they eat at night in those pools. Possibly crayfish, sculpins, and those big caddis larvae. My guess is that the trout are near the pools so they can escape into them, and spend their nights where they spend their days: in the runs but near the pools. That part is a guess. It's not a guess that the largest trout I take from that mile of stream are always caught in the runs between pools but never very far from the pools.

Trout will be found in all small-stream riffles and runs, and even cascades, wherever the water is deep enough to give them some protection from predators and is slowed by some sort of obstruction. Such lies in the fastest water will most often be caused by boulders. Wherever you see a protruding boulder with a slight slick behind it, fish to it. Because boulders can cause the formation of a calm pocket on the upstream side, where the water wells up against it, you'll want to fish both above and below it.

Some steps in mountain streams are so short that the water cascading through them cannot be said to loiter in pools. The water plunges in from upstream, levels out in a bench two to ten feet long, then plunges over onto the next bench. Usually each step has at least one current tongue, sometimes two or three, driving its length. Most often these are too frothed on top to fish well with dry flies, and they're often so tossed that fishing a strike indicator suspending a nymph is just as fruitless.

Almost all of these current tongues have edges that are less violent. You'll notice slight lines of dark water running the length of the whitish current tongue, right alongside it on each flank. That is the seam along which to float your dry fly or to run your suspended nymph. Trout might be holding right under the tongue in water broken by rocks and boulders along the bottom. But they'll be watching the currents for drift, and if the water is less than three feet deep—which it will be in a run in anything that I consider a small stream—they'll have an eye up.

In some stretches of foothill stream, the water might descend for long distances without forming pools at all, flowing instead through what I call deflected runs. The water flows somewhat evenly but is bounced along its course between boulders that are either protruding or completely submerged. Wherever such water is more than a foot or so deep, it might hold trout. Obviously you'll want to fish in relation to those boulders. Place your flies directly upstream and down from them. If the deflected water forms a current of fast water with slower water on both sides, then fish down the line of water that is deeper and faster. If it's so fast that it's bouncy and you have difficulty fishing right down the center of it, then fish its softer edges. That's where trout are most likely to hold anyway, where they can avoid the swift current but dash into it for any food being carried along by it.

Slicks on the surface of any fast water can denote trenches in the bottom. Any time you're walking or wading the water between pools and you notice a bit of dark and smooth surface water surrounded by water that is white and sometimes frothed, fish it. A trout will almost always be found there. If the piece of peaceful water is the only one in a long stretch of water that is too fast for trout to hold, that trout might be a large one.

Pocket water in cascades should be read the same way. Look for bits of dark and somewhat slick water amid the dashing, frothed water. Wherever you find such water, whether it's on a bench or upstream or down from a boulder, fish it with a dry set on top or a nymph tumbled as close to the bottom as you can get it. This will usually require getting right up close to the prospective lie and high-sticking to hold as much line as possible off the surface.

It will usually furnish you some trout you'd not have caught if you just reeled up and prowled from pool to pool. If you're fishing a rushing mountain stream, so steep and fast that more of its water resides in pockets than in pools, you'll catch more trout in the parts between pools than you will in the pools themselves.

CHAPTER EIGHT

An Essential Fly Box

IF YOUR FLY BOXES ARE LIKE MINE, YOU OWN A LOT OF THEM, AND they're all a bit of a tangle. When I'm on a typical trout stream of medium to large size, wearing my vest, its two largest pockets are loaded with a big dry-fly box that has almost innumerable compartments and an outsize nymph box with row after row of flies from tiny and light to some so large and heavily weighted that they go *thump!* when dropped into the palm of the hand. The same two pockets, already full, become overstuffed by two additional boxes of more modest size, one for wet flies and another for streamers.

These four fly boxes, covering the basic categories of trout flies, are far from all I carry. The many peripheral pockets of the vest bulge with smaller boxes for hatches I encounter often: one for midges, a second for *Baetis* mayflies, a third for pale morning duns, a fourth for Tricos, a fifth for . . . sorry, I've run out of time to inventory them. On a trout stream it can take quite a while just to find the right fly box, not to mention the fly I'm after. Sometimes I know I own it but can't ever find it.

Many years ago I recognized that I enjoyed prowling small streams so much, and did it so often to the neglect of what some consider higher forms of fly fishing, that I decided to build a fly box dedicated to the waters I loved most and fished most often. It was foolish to go out onto streams that were often difficult to navigate carrying all that weight and bulk of flies I would never use for that kind of fishing. So I condensed them down to almost nothing.

I bought an Altoids mints tin, ate the candy, and glued in packing foam to hold hooks. This tin held a couple dozen flies, and for some years—most of them my "if they won't take dry flies, they won't take anything" years—I found that they were sufficient for a day spent fishing a small stream. In fact, if I admit the truth, many of my most pleasant seasons were spent carrying nothing but this tiny tin box, a couple spools of spare tippet, a hemostat, a Swiss Army knife with scissors, and a squeeze bottle of floatant to dress the flies and keep them afloat.

Many of my most enjoyable fishing moments during this period came not on the water, but back at the vise after a fishing trip, with that Altoids box open on the bench. Its short rows of dry flies always had a few gaps, revealing which flies had worked best and therefore been left most often in treetops or the jaws of small-stream trout. I tied just enough flies to replace those lost from the gaps in the box. The tying always recalled the pleasant day I'd spent losing the missing flies and brought optimistic thoughts of the next time I'd get out and lose some more.

But I began bumping against days when that little box failed to contain a fly that I needed to solve a certain situation, which is a condensed way to say that some days I was astream among willing trout without a fly that the trout would agree to eat. Those days became more than mildly frustrating.

I remember a particular day on a small stream in Wyoming. It was in the foothills of mountains that stood at some distance, which still had plenty of snow on their tops in late July. The sun was out and bright; the pretty and classic but tiny pools of the stream were shaded in scattered places by overhanging cottonwood trees. The trout were cutthroats. They should have been stupid, willing to dash up for any dry fly.

In a way, they were. I tried my usual first fly in those days, for those types of streams: a size 12 Elk Hair Caddis. Trout rushed it but only splashed it. At first I thought I was too slow in setting the hook. I set myself on a hair trigger and succeeded in blowing the fly out of there faster and more violently, which resulted in catching most of the cottonwoods behind me but still none of the trout in front of me. Then I decided I was striking too quickly, taking the fly away from the trout. I lost fewer flies with patient hook sets but caught no more fish.

Finally I came to the realization that trout were not missing the fly but were turning away from it at the last instant. These were not misses but refusals. Refusals, the formula goes, should always prompt tying on and trying a smaller and less bright fly. I did that. I tried a size 14 Grizzly Wulff, the smallest and darkest fly contained in the very limited selection that little Altoids tin held. That was the day I realized that not only did I not have any size 16 dark dry flies with me while I fished, but there would be no room for them in that tin if I tied them.

I'll not bother you with the fine details of the rest of that day. It was a truly beautiful place to be. I covered quite a bit of water, saw some wondrous sights, surprised some mule deer down to drink, one a buck with velvet on his forming horns. But a day spent fishing is almost always more enjoyable when you catch fish. After that day, I added the drab Deer Hair Caddis, in sizes 12 through 16, to my list of flies to be carried on small streams.

That addition required either leaving something else out of the box or going to a slightly larger one. I traded in the Altoids tin for a small but real fly box, one that would still fit in a shirt pocket but would hold a few more flies.

Since that distant day, I've encountered days when small-stream trout would not address any dry fly, but would happily take a nymph. Reflecting, I realized I'd always had those kinds of days during my dry-fly years; I'd just never armed myself to solve them, so I had no way to know they were happening. I began to carry nymphs.

Then I ran into times when small-stream trout would turn away from drys with a boil but take soft-hackled wets, fished inches deep, with wild abandon. These were among the most pleasant days because fishing soft-hackles upstream forced me to take a position close to pools, so I could see the dart of the line tip that would prompt me to set the hook at the right time. In the clear water of an average small stream, at a range of a few feet, I was able to observe the rushing arrival, turning take, and sudden surprise when a trout felt the hook. It's a thrill to see the splashy strike to a dry fly, but you rarely see the trout, just the results of its swift rise and take. It's ten times the thrill to see the actual take, under the water, to a soft-hackled wet fished a rod length away.

I've enjoyed a few days when a heavy streamer, swept deep, would dig down and bring up fish that refused all else. Some of those trout have been surprisingly large for the size stream I was on, bigger than those I was accustomed to bringing up to dry flies.

My small-stream fly box has grown and gone through many trials and errors because so many fly box types are out there, and I've had to try them all. The one I use now is still not very large. It fits in a typical shirt pocket, though I carry it in the canvas belt bag that so resembles the creel that first banged about my waist.

I strongly recommend that you acquire a medium-size fly box, designate it specifically for your small-stream fishing, and outfit it with a restricted set of flies that is not bulky but arms you for a variety of situations. I like a box with rows of foam to display the flies, so I can quickly locate the pattern and size I'm after, as opposed to a box with open compartments. It's also more fun back at the tying bench, filling in gaps in those rows. The rows need to be ridged, with room for hackles, so you can carry both dry flies and sunk-fly types in that single fly box.

You might prefer two boxes—one with compartments for drys, a second with rows of foam for sunk flies. That's fine. It takes up two shirt pockets or more room in a belt bag, but that is not excessive for flies, which are core to fly fishing. Two boxes allow for a broader selection of flies and might even leave room for expansion, to hold dressings you discover you need to add to your original selection. Expansion within reason is beneficial, when the discussion is flies of any sort. That's the way it should be; you expand your selection to include new flies that work for you out on the water.

I'll be specific about the fly box I use for small streams, since I searched for years and finally found what works, at least for me, at least for now. It's a C&F Design box, plastic, $3^1/2$ by 5 inches, product number CF-150. The inside comes with several options. The one I prefer has eight rows of firm foam rubber with slits along the front of each row, so that you slip the flies into the slits rather than poke them into the foam. The foam doesn't wear out, as most foam does the more it's poked, and therefore it doesn't lose its grip on flies. Each row holds one to two dozen flies, depending on their size. The box holds drys, wets, nymphs, and streamers equally well, displaying them all in neat rows that make it easy to see what options I've got and to pluck out the pattern and size I decide to cast to trout.

In the configuration I prefer for small streams, the box is available with two small lidded compartments—one for split shot, one for strike indicators. If you're happy to carry your shot and indicators separately, the same box also comes configured with twelve rows for flies. This design holds many more flies and might be the better solution. But I prefer a box that limits my options, at least a little, so I don't get confused about fly selection when I'm out on a small stream.

Though I've hinted that fly pattern is not always critical on small streams, that does not mean it's not important to make a careful selection of flies to fish small streams. The reason is simple: Even when trout are willing to take any fly, fly pattern still matters because you want to fish one that you're confident will catch trout and that is easy to see and to keep afloat, assuming it's a dry. When the trout are not willing to take just anything, your careful selection matters much more. You need to have a variety of patterns—surface and sunk—that will most likely include something that resembles what trout have been eating. If you don't, you won't catch many, even on small streams.

When small-stream trout are not fussy about flies, they'll still take more willingly if the fly you show them falls within the range of things they normally eat. Trout might not take a fly that resembles one of their favorite foods any more often than they will something that doesn't, but they will usually take it with more confidence, resulting in more solid hook sets and fewer missed strikes. That's why the most famous flies of the type we call *attractors,* designed to be fished when trout are not feeding selectively, are all based on some common trout food form.

Think about the Royal Wulff, which is said to look like nothing in nature. Its long moose-hair tail, brown hackle collar, and split white calf-tail wings give it the common mayfly shape. Its segmented body of peacock herl and bright red floss turns into a banded body of olive and brown when it gets wet. That's right in the range of natural mayflies, of some beetles, and of many other things that arrive on the surface of trout water.

I agree that the Royal Wulff's white wings are not natural. But I've seen one afloat, submerging myself to look up from beneath the surface, taking the view of the trout, and noticed that the wings are not dominant from that view, especially when you're in a hurry. I was not, until it was time to come up to catch a breath, but small-stream trout are almost always worried that something else will get to a bit of prospective food ahead of them. That puts them in a perpetual hurry.

Trout are not often so rushed that they'll take something far off from what nature offers. But the Royal Wulff is not as far off as we imagine given our view from above. Those white wings help you see it, follow its drift, and notice when a trout takes it. That's half the reason for its success. The other half is its resemblance, from the trout's point of view, to things that land on trout streams and are good for trout to eat.

The Elk Hair Caddis, not an attractor but not often used as an imitative dressing when it's fished on small streams, is another example of a pattern that works so well because it resembles so many things a small-stream trout might eat during its average day. The fly has a tent-shaped wing of elk hair and a hackle palmered over a dubbed body. That's it. One of the reasons it's in so many fly boxes is the ease and speed with which you can tie a bunch. But the Elk Hair Caddis looks like the myriads of tan caddis that hatch on trout streams through summer and into early fall. It's also not a bad imitation for the common yellow sally stoneflies that emerge in late spring and again in fall. It works as a hopper imitation if you've got nothing nearer on you.

The point here is not things the Elk Hair Caddis will imitate exactly. It's the number of things it resembles roughly so that trout recognize it instantly as something providential to eat. It's also easy for you to see, afloat upon trout water.

My own experience with the Elk Hair Caddis on small streams has had its ups, then its downs, then its ups again. At one time, for a long time, it was the first fly I used. I turned to something else only if it failed to take what I considered to be sufficient numbers of trout, which was rare. Then its success began to wane, and I relegated it to a fly I tied on if a Royal Wulff drew refusals. I assigned the Elk Hair's tapering catch to overexposure, which made no sense, because the Royal Wulff has been exposed to small-stream trout a lot longer and still works fine.

The curve of my misfortunes with the Elk Hair Caddis, I discovered a long time later, was related to a mistake I started making when selecting materials to tie it. For many years I tied it as its originator, Al Troth, called for, with a natural tan elk hair wing, a tan body, and ginger hackle. That's the way it worked for me, the way I tied it when it was my first fly.

Then one unlucky day I came across some bleached, and therefore slightly brighter, elk hair in a fly shop. I was excited to get it, because I would be able to see my fly on the water better, and I considered that the critical factor on small streams, where, in those days, I had the philosophy that trout would eat anything. I tied a bunch of Elk Hair Caddis with the brighter hair and indeed was able to see them better. I caught trout on them. I was happy with that change because it was easier to fish.

The flies we carry in our fly boxes can and sometimes should evolve almost unnoticed. Sometimes they should not. I gradually crept toward brighter materials for the wing, body, and hackles on my Elk Hair Caddis. I searched for elk hair that was even more brightly bleached. I used light ginger hackle. I wound the body with synthetic dubbing that was closer to cream than to the original tan. As time went on, I noticed a gradual diminishment in the effectiveness of the old dependable fly. I turned away from it as my first fly. I thought about retiring it but could not.

I can't pin my realization that something had gone wrong with the Elk Hair Caddis on any particular streamside moment. It didn't happen that day in Wyoming when I caught more trees than trout with a bright Elk Hair Caddis. I'm not happy to admit that it was quite a long time later, as I sat on some forgotten streambank, eyed an Elk Hair that had just gotten splashy refusals, noticed how bright it had become. I looked at the row of them in my fly box. They were all the same, all more bright, more showy, than most insects found in nature.

I retired them for that day and for that season. That winter, when I returned to the vise with some time, I refreshed my entire supply with natural elk hair, tan bodies, and medium to dark ginger hackles, just as I'd tied them when the fly was my favorite. Trout began to like it again, and I did too. I'd gotten right back to where the great Al Troth started.

Randall Kaufman's Stimulator started life as an imitation of the golden stonefly. Its tail and down-wing of elk hair, yellow abdomen with grizzly hackle palmered over it, and orange thorax with another palmered grizzly hackle make it an excellent imitation of that large insect seen so often in spring and early summer, making its awkward and almost always fatal descent from the trees to the surface of small trout streams. The fly floats very well. It is easy to see on the water. Like the Elk Hair Caddis, the Stimulator resembles many more things than it was tied to imitate. It looks like a large caddis or moth, a grasshopper, and in the right sizes, many of the larger and lesser pale stonefly species that are close relatives to the golden stones and, like them, so prevalent on small waters.

The Parachute Adams, the version of the famous fly that I find more useful on small waters than the orginal collared-hackle Adams, because it is easier to see, has a moose-hair tail, muskrat fur body, white wing post, and grizzly parachute hackle. I suppose I should tie it with the mixed brown and grizzly hackle the pattern calls for, but I haven't noticed trout turning away from the fly if I leave out the brown hackle, and I have noticed that the fly takes more time to tie with that second hackle added.

That mix of hackle or lack of it, I'm guessing, is one of those divides that separates those who are fly tiers first and fly-fish second from those who are fly fishermen first and tie flies so they can fish with them. If perfection in the fly and devotion to original concepts is your goal, then you should tie the Parachute Adams with mixed brown and grizzly hackle, as you're supposed to. It certainly will not fail you. If you'd like to tie a bunch of flies and get out to the stream with them in a hurry, then you'll tie it with a single grizzly hackle and get going. Wait, I want to go with you.

The Parachute Adams is usually fished in sizes 14 down to 18. Its shape is reminiscent of many medium to small mayflies that trout eat on waters small and large. It might also recall, to trout, the last hatch of midges they got into and gobbled or the minor parade of ants and bee-tles that drop out of streamside brush and trees and float low in the water. The Adams, tied parachute, resembles many things that small-stream trout eat. It's no accident that it fits so well toward the top of the list of any fly selection for small-stream trout.

These basic dry flies in any small-stream trout fly selection—the Royal Wulff, Elk Hair Caddis, Stimulator, and Parachute Adams—are all based on common trout food forms: large mayflies, caddisflies, stone-flies, and back to small mayflies again. Each can also be mistaken by trout for other things that live in and along small streams. Add Ed Schroeder's Parachute Hopper, which is specific for the summer and early-fall grasshopper days that are so common on small desert and meadow streams, and you might have your dry-fly selection rounded out.

Of course, you won't. You'll want to add your favorites, which might be far different from mine. Many folks, for example, will consider it heresy to omit the classic Adams, in its original tie with a hackle col-lar. I can't argue with that. I just don't carry it in my own small-stream selection because it's a bit difficult to see on the water. The parachute version solves that, so I use it instead. I do carry the original Adams for fishing beaver ponds.

Other folks will scold me for omitting the famous Humpy, and they'll clearly be right. With its thick body and carapaced deer-hair back, it can be mistaken by trout for a beetle fallen to the water, a portly mayfly, or a fat-bodied caddis. I've fished with people who have grown up as fly fishers with the Humpy as their favorite searching dry fly, and they consider it foolish to use anything else unless there is clear reason for doing so, which will, in their opinions, be seldom. I've never caught on to tying the complex Humpy quickly. It floats a little low, is a bit hard to see and to keep afloat on frothed water, to have found a favored spot in my own small-stream fly box.

Which flies we favor, or fail to, is often a factor of the success we have with them the first time we fish them. I began fishing small streams with a traditional Royal Coachman. It was a frail fly; its white duck quill wings quickly tattered. The Royal Wulff is a fluffed-out and more heavily hackled hairwing version of the same color scheme. It floats better, shows a lot more buggy profile to trout from below, and is easier, with its thick, white wings, for the angler to see from above. If tied right it's as durable as a tank.

The first time I replaced my Royal Coachman with the brushier Royal Wulff, trout did not accept it any more eagerly than they had the Royal Coachman. But I was able to keep the fly afloat with a lot less trouble, and I was able to notice it when trout took it a lot more often.

It was a robust revolution in my small-stream fishing at that early time, when I was still in my teens. The Royal Wulff got into my fly boxes then, and it rarely fails to fool small-stream trout to this day, so it has never gotten kicked out. Had trout turned up their cold, wet noses to it that first time I tried it, I doubt I'd have given it much chance after that.

A similar success happened to me with a parachute fly that has since found a spot in my scant small-stream selection of dry flies. I did not fish it, but saw it fished the first time by Skip Morris. We were on a bounding mountain stream so small you could step from a mossed rock on one side right over it to another mossy boulder on the other side, at its constrictions. Tangles of vine maple grew over it so tightly that most pools had to be approached on hands and knees. Casts were not often possible; it was almost all dapping.

I fished a Parachute Adams, with its white calf-tail wing, downstream from Skip. The rushing water, dropping from plunge to plunge, created lots of white foam. Flecks of it drifted down the short current tongues of the tiny pools. I had trouble sorting out my fly from its surroundings, even at dapping range. I'd get an occasional hit, but I'd usually be looking at a spot of foam, thinking it was my fly, and the hit would come somewhere nearby. By the time I'd set the hook, the trout would be gone. When you're fishing on your knees because of brush overhead, and you set the hook and miss, the fly goes up into the air, and you know what's next.

After I'd lost a few flies, and not caught any trout, I wandered up to where Skip crouched prayerfully alongside a pool. He was doing the same thing I'd been doing. But I noticed two differences as soon as I got close enough to bring his water into my sight. First, his fly had a yellow wing, which stood out like a little light amid the foam. Second, he could see takes and set the hook, which he did while I watched, launching a trout that was nice for the size water from which it was sprung.

Skip's Parachute has a moose-hair tail, dark olive body, and a dark blue dun hackle wound around a wing post of yellow polypro yarn. I use it in sizes 14 and 16, reserving it for times when its yellow wing will help me sort it out from difficult surroundings.

The Deer Hair Caddis is nothing more than an Elk Hair Caddis with its colors toned down. I tie it more often with gray-dyed yearling elk hair, for small streams, than I do natural gray deer hair, the version I use for bigger waters. The lighter elk hair is a little easier to see on the water, and a little easier to handle when I'm tying. The body is olive, the hackle dark blue dun. Originated by fishing photographer Jim Schollmeyer, the Deer Hair Caddis is excellent on those many small-stream days when trout seem bashful about the brighter Elk Hair Caddis and the Royal Wulff.

The dry-fly side of my small-stream selection is rounded out by a couple of imitative dressings, for use on meadow streams when trout are feeding selectively. The first is the traditional Adams Midge, no more than a grizzly hackle tail, muskrat fur body, and grizzly collar. I carry it in sizes 20 and 22 and hope those will be close enough when trout are feeding on midges or tiny mayflies. It's surprising how often the right size fly will take selective trout, even when the color is far wrong.

The second dry for imitative situations is René Harrop's Olive Hairwing Dun. When trout feed selectively on small mayflies, they're often blue-winged olives, *Baetis,* generally hatching out at size 16 to 20, but sometimes smaller. If the small mayflies that goad trout to selective feeding are not blue-winged olives, a fly in the right size and that color will quite often take trout anyway, especially on small streams, where few fish have master's degrees in aquatic entomology.

The Olive Hairwing Dun serves me very well even on streams where trout have learned to be selective on account of intense fishing pressure. So I carry it in my small-stream fly box, in a range of sizes from 12 down to 20, knowing it will cover accurately everything from big green drakes through lesser green drakes and *flavs* to the tiny blue-winged olives for which it was designed.

The hairwing dun is a modification of the Elk Hair Caddis concept, with split blue dun hackle tails, a slender olive dubbed body, five turns of blue dun hackle spread over the thorax and clipped on the bottom, and a gray calf elk down-wing that is tilted back like the wing on an Elk Hair, but a bit shorter. This shape captures perfectly the silhouette and also the posture of a mayfly dun sitting on the water. The fly floats quite a bit better on wrinkled water than most mayfly dun imitations that are tied for flat water. But the hairwing dun works on water that is flat as well. That's why I prefer it for small streams: It's an excellent imitation, but it will float on the typical water where I'd like to cast it, on either a small meadow stream or a small freestone stream.

That's a limited supply of dry flies, most for searching situations, a few for selective situations. It's enough for me, in most of my small-stream fishing. If I get into a spot where I feel I might need a broader selection of dry flies, it will almost always happen on a miniature meadow stream, where I won't be unhappy to break out my overweight vest, burdened with its full range of fly boxes.

Small streams, except in rare pools, lack the depths attained by larger rivers. Most, though not all, of the nymphs I carry in my small-stream fly box are designed not to get down to the bottom, but to penetrate the surface film far enough to satisfy trout that have some hesitation about taking dry flies up top. This happens often on small streams and is a condition you should be primed to notice because it will vastly affect the outcome of your day if you continue to fish drys when trout continually refuse them.

These days happen most often when it's cool, sometimes drizzly or even raining, and natural insects have their engines set on idle. No aquatics will be hatching. No terrestrials will be rambling around in brush or treetops, risking fatal falls. Trout don't see anything on the surface to eat. Their attention is not turned up there. They continue to feed on the drift down below, and that is where they focus.

Sometimes trout refuse to take on top even when the sun is out and bright. One of the philosophies handed to me in my youth was that *fly fishing is best when the sun is on the water.* That adds up to sense when you consider that my fly-fishing mentors used only dry flies. Drys fish best when trout are actively engaged in feeding on the surface. That happens most often on small streams when insects are warmed up, either hatching from the water or falling to it from streamside vegetation. When the sun is on the water, insects are most active, and trout have their attention turned up. They're a little like sprinters crouched at the blocks, waiting for the snap of the starter's pistol. They're down in their lies, most often along the bottom, but the bottom is not far from the surface, and they've got their eyes up there, their fins braced against the water, ready to race the instant something touches down.

On some bright days, for reasons largely left to guessing, small-stream trout are bashful about the surface, even if insects are out and risking trouble. Trout seem still to be on their starting blocks. They initiate that dash. Then they turn away at the last second. They see something that frightens them. You see a splash and set the hook. It blows out of there. You know the rest.

I have a couple of guesses. The first is that trout are afraid, at times, to expose themselves to overhead predation. If a kingfisher is fresh in a trout's memory, the trout might get more anxious the nearer it approaches total exposure at the surface. So it gets timid, turns away, makes a splash. That's a stretch because when they're bashful about the top, it's all of them, not just one of them.

Trout risk predation on small streams, or they starve. How would you feel if a monster lived on your roof, looked down through a skylight at your dinner table, and got primed for action every time the table got set? You'd display some anxiety as you took your accustomed seat. But if you lived in a small stream, were even the boss of your pool, you'd still take your seat. You'd just be real ready to leap out of it.

I don't even believe myself when I postulate that small-stream trout turn away from drys, on bright days, because of fear from overhead predation. But I also don't pretend I know how trout think, so I include it among the possibilities.

A more likely possibility is that a trout, launched on its rush toward a dry fly floating on the surface, suddenly recognizes that what it's about to eat is not food. So it turns away at the last second. You see a boil or a splash, depending on how near the trout got before it realized it had made a mistake. You set the hook and succeed in nothing more than ripping your fly off the water. I believe this is most often the cause for refusals, though I don't know why this kind of refusal happens most often on bright days.

I had an example of this laid out plainly for me once, by entire accident. I was hiking in to the headwaters of a coastal stream, heading for a waterfall above which I'd find my favorite resident cutthroat trout, below which were blocked the fish that used the same stream at other times of year: winter steelhead, fall coho, chinook salmon, all eager to spawn. I reached a point where I had to wade across a tributary of the stream before continuing along the abandoned road I was hiking. Before I crossed, I dropped my backpack, loaded with supplies for a three-day stay up where I wanted to be, and took a rest.

The old road had bridged the branch in some distant past, but a thunderous winter flood had driven the logs of the bridge downstream, probably flushed them all the way out to the ocean, not far away to the west. It left exposed what would have been a bridge pool had there still been a bridge. The road, no longer used by anything but deer, bear, elk, and occasional anglers, was grassed right up to the bank, which stood a few feet above that pool. I sprawled there, bellied right up to the edge, and peered over. Trout were down there.

They were small, perhaps half a dozen of them, the biggest half a dozen inches long. They hovered over the clean gravel, lit by the sun. They were easy to see, and it was easy to see that they were somewhat nervous on account of their exposure. But that is likely the natural condition of trout in small streams: somewhat nervous. Maybe they were just momentarily nervous because they'd seen my head poking from the bank, into their view, but I don't think they saw me, because they didn't settle down while I lay there watching them. Their fins quivered and their tails twitched, driving them a foot or two to one side or other of the lies to which they always returned.

My own lie was over a fallen alder limb; it was uncomfortable under my ribs. I pulled it out, noticed it had a lacework of tiny twigs attached, idly broke off an inch the thickness of a matchstick, lobbed it onto the water of the pool, a few feet upstream from those trout. The biggest one, followed by two or three others, left its bottom lie instantly, speared up toward that bit of twig. The biggest got there first but turned away when it got within inches, leaving a boil that engulfed the twig. Had I been fishing the pool with a dry fly, watching its float from casting distance, even short, I'd have set the hook.

The trout all returned to their lies. I waited awhile, tossed out another inch of twig. The same thing happened, except this time the biggest trout wasn't in the biggest hurry, and two of the smaller trout got to the twig first. They missed it with a heck of a splash. One came right out of the water, flung out by its own momentum. I thought I heard it roar. Had I been fishing, I'd have set the hook again.

I viewed this as rare instruction, lay there for a long time, flipping twigs and watching the reaction of the trout. The largest two or three of them tired of the game soon, but the smallest of them, four- and five-inchers, were never able to subdue their urge to rush up for those twigs. When I reduced the size of the twigs to a quarter inch or so, smaller than the average size fly I fish on small streams, they began to take them down, mouth them, then let them go. I'd have hooked those and probably would have caught them. I might even have been proud.

An epiphany arrived: When trout boil a fly or splash it, and you set the hook but miss, it's not your fault for the way you strike. It's a refusal. It's your fault for fishing a fly the trout don't want. Two obvious solutions offer themselves. The first is to go to a dry fly that is smaller and drabber. My automatic first move, in a situation where trout refuse a Royal Wulff, Elk Hair Caddis, or Stimulator, is to nip the big, bright fly off, add a couple feet of finer tippet, usually 5X added to the 4X that is already on there, and tie on a size 16 Parachute Adams.

If that doesn't work, and there are many days that it does not, then I usually switch to a nymph.

Most of the nymphs in my box, as I began by saying, are designed not to dredge the bottom but to penetrate the surface. I've found that those trout already looking upward and willing to feed, but for some reason either bashful about the surface or not convinced that the dry fly I set there for them represents food, will almost always accept a nymph fished shallow. They'll have no trouble noticing it because their attention will be focused up to the top. They'll normally not be bashful about walloping it.

A few favorite nymphs have found seats in my small-stream fly box. I don't necessarily recommend them to you because you've probably got your own favorites, and there is little doubt yours will work better for you. Again, it goes back to what has worked well in your past and therefore promises that it will work in your future.

My favorite nymph is an Olive Beadhead I tied because I could not find one in that color that is so common in natural aquatic insects. It's the same dressing that worked well during a serendipitous rappelling of green inchworms into a small-stream pool, beneath a conifer bough. Like the best dry flies, it resembles many of the things that small-stream trout eat, including the abundant caddis larvae commonly called green rockworms. Those riffle-dwelling insects, varying from drab olive to bright green, are rarely absent from a kick-net sample taken from the fastest water of any small stream.

This Olive Beadhead has a bright dubbed abdomen, yellow thread rib, darker hare's mask fur thorax, and gold or brass bead. I've not noticed that the color of the bead matters. Some folks speculate that a bead makes a nymph more effective than one tied without it because it helps get the fly down deeper and faster. I've not had any trouble getting a nymph down deep and fast with lead wire wrapped around the hook. I believe beadheads are more often effective because that bit of flash attracts the attention of trout.

It's also true that many aquatic insects, when about to emerge, exude gases that become trapped between the outer skin of the immature stage and the inner skin that enwraps the soon-to-erupt adult stage. These gases reflect light. A beadhead on a nymph does the same thing. Beads are pinpoints of light to attract and deceive those small-stream condensations of light that we call trout.

If that sounds like a lot of baloney, don't doubt that beadhead nymphs work. If your favorite nymph is a Gold-Ribbed Hare's Ear, which is a fine one, try adding a bead and fishing the two on the same leader, on a small stream. I'll be surprised if your results come out anywhere near even. But I might be wrong. And you might abhor the idea of adding a bright bead to a nymph. I have friends who declare that is no longer imitative. I explain to them that in my opinion, the flash of the bead represents the gases trapped under the skin of a natural and that, therefore, the fly might be more imitative. I won't distress you with the language they've used to tell me what they think about that crazy idea.

I carry this beadhead in sizes 12 to 16 and use it most often on small streams in the midrange of those sizes: 14. It is my searching nymph, counterpart to the Royal Wulff or Elk Hair Caddis dry, which I choose between at will, depending more on my mood than on any conditions on the stream.

A second favorite nymph, tried sometimes in response to failure of the Olive Beadhead, other times when I notice a scattering of green drake mayflies on the water and in the air above it and know the nymphs of that big beast are restless, is André Puyan's A. P. Black. I actually arrived at this fly on my own, as I have some others, but realized in tying it one day that it was such a logical arrangement of materials that somebody else had probably invented it ahead of me. On checking, I discovered that to be true. The A. P. Black has a moose body-hair tail, black fur abdomen, and dark turkey quill shellback over a thorax of more black dubbing, picked out fuller than the abdomen. That's it. If you collected some green drake nymphs and took them home, set them next to your tying vise, tied something simple to match their blocky bodies, that's what you'd end up with, too.

This fly should be moderately weighted for fishing small streams, specifically with eight turns of lead wire the diameter of the hook shank. You want it to sink quickly when it hits the water, but you don't want it to plop to the bottom and remain in one place.

When I want a nymph to do some dredging on a small stream, which admittedly is very rarely, I use Charlie Brooks's Montana Stone. It's an imitation of the giant salmon-fly nymph, but in my experience, on a lot of streams of all sizes in a lot of places across this big continent and around this little world, it's an excellent searching fly, even in waters that lack salmon flies. I abbreviate the great man's pattern, to make it easier to tie, and tie it on smaller hooks—long-shank size 10s and 12s—than he did.

The fly begins with about twenty to twenty-five wraps of lead wire, layered under the abdomen and double-layered under the thorax. It is designed to sink quickly. The tails are forked goose-wing biots, the body and thorax black fur or yarn. A hen grizzly hackle and a gray ostrich herl fiber are tied in together at the end of the abdomen, then wound forward in just two or three turns over the thick thorax. The hackle and ostrich represent roughly the gills and legs of the natural. The entire operation roughly represents something big, black, ugly, and alive, thumping along the bottom of the fastest small-stream water types.

It works. That's about it for nymphs.

I carry size 16 and 18 Serendipity nymphs in olive and red, plus Flashback Pheasant Tail Nymphs in sizes 18 through 22, mostly in case I discover a need to be imitative on a small meadow stream or spring creek. Often a tiny nymph will take trout on such waters when everything else fails. It would not be wise to omit tiny flies entirely, even for a small-stream selection. When you need them, there will be no substitutes. When size is critical, it's surprising how often shape and color are not.

I do carry other nymphs in my small-stream fly box, on account of my consideration that beaver ponds and isolated woodland ponds are likely to be encountered by the person who prowls small streams, and it's wise to be able to fish them with some hope of success. These pond nymphs include the TDC, a midge pupa pattern with a black body, silver wire rib, and white ostrich herl head. Tied in sizes 14 through 18, it matches many common midge species in their most important stage. If midges are not present, the TDC, which was originated by biologist Dick Thompson and stands for Thompson's Delectible Chironomid, seems to remind stillwater trout about them. Beaver pond trout often take it willingly when nothing is around to predict its success.

I also carry slightly weighted scud dressings, no more than fur bodies and shellbacks of Ziploc bag material ribbed with the working thread, in size 14 and in four colors: orange, pink, gray, and olive. The olive gets used most, because most scuds take on the color of the vegetation among which they live. But the others make the small-stream fly box somewhat colorful, and that's important, even if it means nothing to trout in small waters.

My own small-stream selection is rounded out by a very narrow list of wet flies and streamers. I carry the Partridge and Yellow soft-hackled wet, in sizes 12 and 14, because I had some astonishing success on it the first time I tried it on a favorite home stream. I was fishing up close in its tiny pools on a day when trout were bashful about the surface. I found they would accept the bright soft-hackle as eagerly as they had been refusing drys. I also found that I could follow the bright fly, drifting along just a few inches beneath the surface, and sometimes mark takes to it by the simple fact of its sudden disappearance.

The trout blended into the background of the pools in which they lived. They'd move up invisibly and inhale the fly. All I'd notice was that the fly was no longer there. When I'd set the hook, a trout would be on. It was like magic then, and still is. The Partridge and Yellow, the way I tie it for small streams, consists of two layers of Pearsall's Gossamer silk thread for the body and two turns of speckled gray partridge for the hackle. That's it. It doesn't take long to tie a season's supply.

I also carry a few wet Alders, with peacock herl bodies, black hackles, and dark mottled turkey quill wings, size 12. They're handy at rare times on small streams when trout feed on the adults that descend from streamside trees. Because alderflies are unable to float, they subside at once and are taken subsurface. The Alder is more important for ponds, because the predaceous larvae of the natural alderfly are more abundant in the leaf packs of stillwater bottoms.

I carry a few Muddlers, in size 10 and unweighted, because sculpins are so prevalent on small streams, and trout like to hunt them across the sweeps of shallow tailouts. When trout are doing that, or when they are just hanging on tailouts, exposed and so flighty that it's almost impossible to approach them from downstream and cast a dry fly up to them without spooking them, then it's often wise to take a position near the head of a pool, set a Muddler to one edge of the tailout, and swim it across. You'll see those arrows well up. Often they will shoot right to your fly. Don't set the hook too soon. That will send the arrow off in the wrong direction and set the entire pool on edge.

I carry Olive Lead-Eye Woolly Buggers, in size 10, to dredge bottoms of deep and frothed runs and also deep and dark pools. I use them rarely and feel guilty whenever I do. But they've taken trout for me, over the years, on waters from Soda Butte Creek in Yellowstone Park to a small spring creek in Missouri that I was led to and allowed to fish without ever being told where I'd been taken. I'll get into that story in the chapter on streamers.

That's all of them. It's not many flies, but they fill a medium-size fly box to bursting. That's the way I like it. There's little room for expansion but enough options that I know something in there will take trout in all but the most exceptional small-stream situations. When I bump into those, then I know it's time to add a pattern or two. But I always have the fear that the selection will become too broad and will necessitate going back to that full range of fly boxes I carry in my vest. I don't want that to happen. That's why I like the minor restrictions of the single fly box that I carry for all of my small-stream fly fishing, no matter where my travels take me.

This box, tied to completion, with all the gaps in its rows filled and a few other flies poked in the foam outside the rows, where they don't belong, has some beauty. Small-stream trout are beautiful; that's a lot of why we fish for them. Small streams themselves are beautiful; that might be the most of why we fish them. The more beauty we can take to them, in the form of the rods we carry, the creel or belt bag or whatever we wrap around us, and the flies we fish while on the water, the more fun we'll have while we're out there.

The presence of beauty might even cause us to catch more trout as well, but that would be difficult to prove.

CHAPTER NINE

Trout on Drys

IT'S NO ACCIDENT THAT DRY FLIES WORK WELL ON SMALL STREAMS more often than they do on midsize streams and large rivers. The reasons are real and easy to understand once you think about that confined environment in which small-stream trout make a living eating mostly insects and occasionally other stuff.

The bottom of a small stream is rarely a long trip from its top. Depth is relative to size of the stream. A few deep pools in small streams are carved down to six feet, sometimes even ten feet. But the deepest pools are usually no more than three to five feet deep, and most holding lies in riffles, runs, and pocket water are even shallower than that. Prodded to guess, I'd say that the abundance of trout, holding in lies along the bottom of most small waters, is consistently within two to three feet of the surface, often less than that.

Even the deepest parts of small-stream pools are usually shallow enough for trout to look up and spot insects, or dry flies, drifting on surface currents. In water that is deeper than five to six feet, trout are less likely to spend time looking upward and are not as likely to be able to see something on the surface when they do. When trout have just two to four feet to move from the bottom to the top, it's a short enough distance that the quick trip to nip whatever is up there will cost less energy than is gained by getting it, assuming it's an insect rather than your dry fly.

That formula changes in medium trout streams and larger rivers. They tend to have more deep water than small streams, and those depths tend to be deeper. Where the water is shallow, say in a riffle, trout in big water are almost as likely to feed on top as trout in small water. But small streams have a higher percentage of shallow lies, and therefore a larger percentage of trout willing to take dry flies whenever they get shown them. Trout in larger waters tend to feed on top in response to a hatch or terrestrial fall and keep their attention focused on bottom drift when nothing in numbers attracts that attention upward. When they're not looking up, they're not as susceptible to dry flies.

Small streams are also more productive for fishing dry flies, more often than larger waters, because terrestrial life that falls to a stream surface increases as a proportion of total trout provisions as the width of the stream decreases. On a wide river, terrestrials get into trouble with trout only along the edges. A few hoppers, beetles, or flying ants might get carried by the wind far out to midstream currents, but not very often in sufficient numbers to keep a trout's belly full. As the streamcourse gets narrower, the percentage of food falling to the surface from vegetation along the banks and overhead gets greater. The more food that arrives from above, the more time trout spend with their attention turned up to the surface, where dry flies float.

On a small stream hemmed in by brush and overhung by limbs and branches, the entire surface area of the stream is equivalent to the narrow strip of bank water along a larger river. It's likely that in summer and early fall, when terrestrial life is most abundant, almost as much food falls to trout from above as they find in the drift along the bottom below.

Not all insects that fall to small streams are terrestrials. Small streams, and the edges of medium and big ones for that matter, frequently have what I call *brush hatches*. These might be terrestrial insects either falling or flying out of streamside vegetation, getting onto the surface, getting eaten by trout. Just as often they're flights and falls of aquatic insects, emerging as adults out of the brush rather than as immatures out of the water. Mating and egg-laying dances of mayflies are examples. So are erratic dispersal flights of caddisflies and patient but fatal helicopter descents of egg-laden stoneflies.

Brush hatches increase in importance as streams diminish in size. They attract trout's attention upward. They increase the effectiveness of dry flies on small streams.

Small streams are excellent for searching with dry flies because narrow waters tend to show trout a wide variety of things to eat, and therefore they have fewer reasons to become selective. Aquatic insects adapt to specific niches. The various kinds of niches in a small stream, such as spaces between bottom stones in riffles, algal pastures on faces of bigger boulders in runs, leaf packs on the bottoms of pools, are all closer together than the same kinds of niches on larger streams and rivers. That nearness of niches causes trout to see the wide array of insects that might hatch from all types of aquatic environments, sometimes in a single day or even hour.

Trout holding in lies on larger water, say a big riffle or broad flat, are more likely to see large numbers of a single aquatic insect species, all coming off at once, than they are to see a wide variety of things, all mixed up. Add the broad range of terrestrial insects that fall to the surfaces of small streams, and you have trout that would reduce their own chances for survival if they got selective very often.

Brook trout and cutthroats are often referred to as stupid because they become selective least often, rainbows less stupid because they are selective more often, and we all know that brown trout are smart because they're almost always selective. In a sense that might approach being true. Brown trout, from Europe, have been fished over for enough trout generations that it's quite possible they've refined their sense for separating something good to eat from something that might sting them if they eat it. Brookies and cuts had never been fished over, at least with flies, before Europeans arrived on our continent. Because they had never seen flies, they did not learn to avoid them.

The willingness of so-called stupid trout to rush and take almost anything that gets in their gunsights might not be due to a lack of education. It's more likely a response to the swifter and less rich headwater environments in which both brookies and cuts evolved, compared with those of rainbows and browns. They might have starved themselves into extinction had they behaved any other way. That would have been stupid.

Brook trout and cuts in small streams adapted over eons to their varied environment by learning to be first to food. The instinct to race their relatives, coupled with the tendency to take something in and try it, spit it out if it turned out not to be nutritious, was shaped over many more generations than man has had to hone the sensibilities of brown trout by fishing for them with flies.

A small-stream brook trout or cutt that became a picky feeder would not last long and would not pass its genes on to any next generation. Rainbow trout, placed into the same restrictive situation, behave in the same way or starve. Brown trout in small streams might be more cautious than brook trout or cutthroats. In our anthropomorphic terms, that makes them smarter. In terms of survival of the species, if they carry that caution so far that they starve, it makes them stupid.

Brown trout are not stupid. Given a few generations to adapt to life in a small stream, they are smart enough to behave about the same as any other trout species in the same environment. They race to take dry flies just as eagerly as brookies, cutts, and rainbows.

Small-stream trout hold in lies not far from the top. They see a wide variety of trout foods land on the surface. They often race to take them before anybody else gets to them. Those three factors, added together, create in small streams the ideal environment for the dry fly. Given that, how do you fish dry flies on small streams?

It's almost always best to move upstream along small streams. Trout hold facing into the current, watching for whatever food the current might deliver. Trout can't see behind them as well as they can see in front of them. If your approach is from downstream, behind them, it's not so difficult to slip up on them. If you attempt to approach from upstream, you'll move right into their sight. You'll have to keep your body a lot lower, and also tilt your rod constantly to the side, to keep its sudden movement, and that of the line and leader, from frightening them.

When you wade upstream toward trout, anything you kick up from the bottom is delivered directly downstream by the current, away from the trout you're stalking. If you wade downstream toward trout, anything you kick up will drift ahead of you, at least alert them, perhaps alarm them. You're not likely to dislodge logs or even sticks. But you will disturb the streambed. Any silt or even scents released from it will move along ahead of you. Sometimes the message you send moves along invisibly, spoiling your fishing without any hint about why you're suddenly not catching anything. If you find it necessary to move downstream on small water, wade as little as possible, and stay out of the water and up on the banks as much as you can.

When you fish upstream on a small stream, it makes sense to take a position at the lower end of whatever kind of water you're about to fish, and to cast over its holding lies in order, from those closest to you first to those farthest away last. This amounts to a sort of warning against something I've already recommended: high-grading pools for the largest trout. If you approach a pool, read its water, determine the most likely lie for the biggest fish, then make your first cast right there, you'll often catch it. If you must make that first cast over lies that are likely to hold smaller trout, however, those smaller trout will see your line shoot overhead. They'll dive into the safest place in the pool, which will almost certainly be right where that big one is holding.

Fright is contagious. When one or two small trout dive into its hide, you're not likely to get the big one to show any interest in your fly.

Most of the time, you should work your way up a pool, fishing all the likely water as you come to it. If catching small trout seems a bother to you, perhaps you're on the wrong type of water. But there's also the strong chance that small-stream lies you expect to provide tiddlers will spring fairly large surprises on you. Don't pass up the water lower down in a pool to fish the better water higher up unless you have reason to believe that the lowest lies are empty of trout.

If the pool you're about to fish has a bouldered tailout, then your first casts should cover it. Trout will hold right in front of the fastest water, where it begins the drop into the next pool, if there is any depth there and any rocks or boulders big enough to break the current. Sometimes tailout trout will tuck themselves right in at the edges, next to the fast current, in soft side pockets where the current is broken by crevices in the boulders or trenches in the bottom.

You'll have trouble getting a good float with a dry fly on gathering tailout currents. As the water narrows from the width of the pool above and funnels toward the drop into the pool below, it accelerates. The water at the upper end of a tailout, nearest to the pool, is slower than the water farther down the tailout, toward its exit. If you take the most common position, straight downstream, a cast from there will lay your line and leader directly upstream onto the tailout. The fly, up high, will drift slowly. The line, down low, will get grabbed by the current and be whisked right along. Your leader will come tight to the fly almost at once and begin to drag your fly downstream.

Even if you manage to cast straight up onto a tailout with some slack in the line and leader, the accelerating current will straighten your leader quickly, and your fly will begin to race after a drift of just a couple of feet, sometimes less than that. The best way to defeat the constant problem of drag on a tailout is to creep up and take a position as close to the tailout as you can, either bent over or even on your knees. Use the boulders of the tailout to conceal your approach. Try to get just a little more than a leader length away from the water you'd like to fish. Then you can drop your fly and leader onto the water and, by lifting your rod high, hold most of your line above the swift current. You'll get a longer drag-free float.

Don't make any casting movements abruptly when you're that close to trout. The key, in a close approach to a tailout, is to keep yourself out of sight, and keep your rod movements so slow that they don't attract the attention of trout and remind them about the last kingfisher that arrived with a flash and a splash. Keep your footfalls light. Don't bang any rocks together. Those types of low-frequency alarms get transferred through the water and detected by the lateral lines of the trout. They'll flee.

If protruding boulders form the likely lies on a tailout, which is often the case on small freestone streams, you can use the same boulders to defeat drag. Take your initial position a few feet downstream from the tailout, just far enough off to one side so that your cast will lie over rocks and not land on rushing water. Place the fly a foot or two upstream from the lie you expect to hold a trout. Aim the delivery stroke so that the line drapes itself over a boulder. The line will hold up on the boulder. You'll get a long enough float to give trout a chance to make a decision about your fly. They don't need a long float, but they do need to see the fly floating freely rather than racing.

When a trout makes a decision to take your dry fly on a cast that you've draped over a boulder or a bunch of them on the bank, you might find that the cast itself has put you in trouble. If all goes well, when you set the hook, you'll lift the line right off the rocks, using the resistance of the trout itself as leverage, and avoid any problems. Sometimes not all goes precisely so well. Your line will often get stuck under the edge of a rock, or on a twig or branch that you've not noticed. If that happens, give the rod a quick shake, see if you can free the line. If it won't come loose, you're in for an adventure.

That's one of the most important things you're after whenever you fish a small stream: adventure. Do whatever you can to free the line but recall that without that cast, you'd never have hooked the trout and had that minor mishap, which will become fun by the time you think about it later, whether or not you manage to catch the trout.

Trout must make their decisions on tailouts almost instantly. If something lands on top of their heads they either are frightened by it or spear up to attack it. Consider that potential reaction in your cautious approach to the tailout of a pool and in the way you make your fly arrive in front of the trout you expect to be holding there. If you expose yourself on your way into position, trout will dash away. If you wave your rod right over the tailout, you'll observe V-wakes arrowing up the pool. If your fly lands with a smash, a small flock of trout might bolt downstream right between your feet, bumping against your wadered legs in their hurry to get out of there. That is the ultimate expression of disapproval: trout running into you in their rush to run away from you.

Whenever you fish a small-stream tailout, get as close as you can without alerting trout to your presence, keep low, cast short, and place your dry fly on the water as softly as you can. Be careful about drag, and you'll catch trout.

In the chapter on reading water, I pointed out that most trout spend most of their time in some relation to the current tongue that delivers the main force of the flow down the length of an average small-stream pool. If boulders break the flow beneath a current tongue, trout hold in lies directly in the center of it. If there are no sheltered lies right under a current tongue, trout hold off to the softer edges of it, in position to rush up to take whatever might be delivered down its surface.

The flow of a current tongue has more force and is therefore more chopped on top in the center than it is off to the sides. The surface also has more bounce, higher waves, and more white water the farther up the current tongue you go toward the head of the pool. Trout are able to see things drifting on the surface better at the lower ends and the edges of current tongues, less well as they hold farther up toward the head of the current and closer to its center. When most of their food arrives from overhead, on the surface, rather than down below, as part of the drift, this is a very good reason for trout to hold a bit out of the central current, where they can get a better view of what passes down the length of it. It's also a reason you should explore the lower end of the current tongue first, and then its edges, before you float your dry fly right down its center.

After fishing a tailout thoroughly, which usually takes just a few casts on account of those quick decisions trout must make there, it's time to move into position to fish the lower end of the current tongue in the body of the pool. On many small streams, this does not require a move at all. You just aim your cast farther up the pool. On most small-stream pools, it requires moving up alongside the tailout, or even wading right up into it. Keep your cautions in mind. If your new position is close to where you feel trout might hold at the downstream end of the current tongue, stay low and tilt your rod into a sidearm cast. And never send wading waves over trout you'd like to catch. That alerts them, sometimes alarms them. Either way, it makes it difficult to catch them.

If your position is directly downstream from the current tongue, fan your casts up into its lower end. Since the largest trout is most likely to lie right where the central current plays out into deep water, set your fly in position to drift down that line over that lie first. Many pools will be nearly still where the current peters out. Don't lift your fly off such water until you feel trout have had ample time to consider its presence up there. They don't make the same swift decisions in slow water that they do where it's fast.

Repeat your casts over that most likely lie at least a couple of times, more if the water is deeper than four feet or so. You want to give trout more than one chance. It's also possible that a trout of some size, seeing something pass over its head three or four times, might decide a hatch or terrestrial fall is commencing, and it had better get active. We are not able to tell precisely how trout do their thinking in such situations, but it's not news that a trout might rise to the fourth or fifth cast after refusing all those ahead of it.

After fishing the line of drift directly upstream from you, essentially in the center of the current tongue, then fan your casts to both sides of it. Again, repeat each drift at least a time or two to give trout a chance to make up their minds.

If your initial position is off to the side of the current tongue, rather than directly downstream in line with the flow, then you'll need to fish it a bit differently. Place your first casts on the side nearest you, beginning where the current loses its force. Extend subsequent casts across this lowest end of the current tongue, covering a foot or, at most, two of new water as you cover lines of likely lies with parallel drifts. Watch the drift of your dry fly carefully. If any drag sets in, either shift your position to make your casts more directly upstream, into the current, or make an upstream mend by flicking your rod up and over, lifting the line off the water and laying it over into an upstream curve on the water.

After you've fished the lower end of a current tongue from side to side, then it's time to move up and fish the inside edge of the tongue. The best position will be one straight downstream that therefore lets you cast directly up into the current, because that is the cast that lets the downstream drift of the fly, directly toward the rod, remove any chance of drag from a tight line and leader.

A current tongue that flows down the center of a pool will be straight and will decrease in speed as it dissipates its force. Link those two factors—a straight current, slowing as it goes—and it's easy to see why this might be the best place in any stream to fish with basic casts made directly upstream, with no slack in the line or the leader. The natural drift of the line, leader, and fly downstream toward you will insert slack into the drift.

This is the most straightforward bit of fishing you'll do on any small stream. Since it will often be the bulk of it, you can see why you're going to have no trouble retaining your happiness, as measured by trout hooked and handled, as you move toward more experience and subsequent solutions to the more complex parts of an average pool.

When fishing a current tongue from one side, which you will be forced to do on most small-stream pools, your line naturally lands on the water nearest you, which is slow, while your fly lands on the current tongue itself, always faster. This is a perfect prescription for drag. You can combat it to a certain extent with your casting. If you're able to execute a curve cast, by either under- or overpowering a sidearm delivery stroke, then you can lay the line straight out from the rod on the slower currents, and hook the line tip and leader upstream on the faster currents. The fly drifts freely down toward the line tip, and you'll get several feet of float before any drag has a chance to set in.

Another way to cast to a current tongue from off to the side, without getting drag as your dry fly drifts back down the length of it, is to wade cautiously as near to the current as you can, then make your delivery stroke sidearm, with your rod arm extended full length, so the line, out there the distance of your arm and rod from you, lays out right up the length of the current tongue. Then your drift is right back down toward the rod tip, out over the current. A caution when you take this approach: Extend each cast up into the current tongue just the length of your leader longer than the cast before it. That way you'll get a drift the length of your leader in which trout have not been exposed to the line flying over their heads.

If you wade in and make your first cast the entire length of the current tongue, your line will fly over the full length of the water you'd like to fish. Trout in all but the last few feet, up there under the leader, will be lined. Your only information about this is a lack of success. Lined trout rarely rise to take dry flies. Whenever you cast a dry fly straight up into a current tongue, make your measuring forecasts off to one side. Make each delivery in a way that causes your fly to fish just a leader length of new water each time, no more.

Wherever it's possible, move into a position that allows you to fish directly up into a current tongue. That lets you fish the near side, the center, and the far side of the current tongue without the need for curve casts or any other trickery to defeat drag.

It's not a guess that a dragging fly will be ignored by small-stream trout most of the time. I took a steelhead fisherman to one of my favorite small streams not long ago. He was enthralled by the possibility of catching cutthroat trout in summer in the headwaters of the same stream he fished lower down, below a waterfall, for winter steelhead. But he regarded the resident cutts as he might summer steelhead or sea-run cutts and fished his dry fly with constant movement to draw them to it.

We skipped pools, each of us fishing every other one, a great way to divide up a small stream and still keep close to the company you've taken there. I did fine, caught fish where I expected to, none where I did not. The stream was full of trout, and they were quite willing to whack dry flies that pleasant summer day. I was focused on my own fishing and failed to notice that my friend was not doing very well until he was suddenly standing behind me, neglecting his own fishing, watching what I was doing. That prompted me to get behind him at the next pool, watch what he was doing, and see if I could help, which is what I should have done in the first place. As a host, I'm eager to attend to my own fishing and only offer help if my focus is intruded upon.

The steelhead fisherman had no trouble reading the small pool he was about to fish, a long one with a brisk current tongue. He took his position on a gravel bar on the shallow side of the main flow and placed his first cast right to where I would have expected the nicest trout to hold, where the current tongue calmed down and flattened a bit over the deepest water in the pool. I anticipated the splash of a take. I was surprised instead to see that as soon as his dry hit the water, before any trout could get to it, my friend lifted his rod tip to tug the fly into a skate of a foot or so. Then he dropped the rod tip, let the fly float along about the same distance before raising the rod tip again, skating the fly a foot or so more.

A boil behind his fly revealed that a trout had seen it, investigated it, rejected it. Apparently the trout was frightened by it, because it would not even boil the fly on a bunch of following casts to the same bit of water with the same fly movement.

I was caught between wanting to be polite, and therefore remain silent, and the desire to have this steelheader do well over my favorite little trout. I finally told him that in my experience, once a fly moved in any way under the inducement of the leader to which it was tied, that cast was defeated, and it was time to get the fly off the water and make another cast onto different water.

He picked up that cast, walked ten feet upstream alongside the pool, while carrying his line gracefully in the air, and set his fly farther up the current tongue. He let it drift slowly down the edge of the flow without imparting any movement. A trout rushed the fly and took it with a smack.

Fishing the near side and center of a current tongue is relatively straightforward, not often difficult. But the far side of the current is just as likely to hold trout as the near side. Perhaps it's more likely to hold a nice trout, since it gets fished without drag less often than the near side. If the depth of the water and the circumstances of scenery surrounding the pool allow you to wade straight upstream, and thereby fish both sides and the center of the current tongue with casts straight upstream and drifts straight back down, then you'll be able to fish both sides equally well. In the more common case, where you must approach the pool from one side and fish the inside, center, and outside of the current tongue from one position, life gets more difficult.

It's tough to fish over the top of a current tongue, to the far side, without getting drag. Most of the solution lies in getting as close to the current as you can. If that position is about a rod length from the far current, you'll be able to cast up onto that edge, lay the leader and line tip onto the water in the same set of currents behind the fly, and get a good drift by lifting your rod high enough to hold the back part of your line above the water. It's critical that all the line and leader on the water lie in the same set of currents and, therefore, travel downstream at the same speed. If the faster central current gets ahold of the back end of the line while your fly floats on slower currents on the far side, the line will speed up and cause drag.

If you're not able to get close enough to the currents to hold the back end of the line off the water, you'll have to deal with drag in a different way. The most successful method I've found is to cast across the current with a bit of an upstream curve in the leader, then expect a very short drift. The back of the line will take that curve out after the fly has traveled just two to three feet. So I fish the outside edge of the current tongue in two- to three-foot increments. Each time, I lift the fly off the water the instant it begins to drag. Then I place it back onto the water a couple of feet upstream from the place it landed on the previous cast.

In this way, the fly fishes fresh water a couple of feet at a time. It might not seem like much, but it's enough to cover the length of an average small-stream pool in ten to no more than twenty casts.

Even if you have not yet mastered curve casts, you can cover the far edge of a current tongue with casts straight across the tongue and get one- to two-foot drifts. Just be sure you've covered all the nearer water before you start sending casts sailing over there and then dragging your fly back across the central current.

Always calculate your casts, on any bit of small-stream trout water, so that your fly is fishing over water where trout have not seen it dragging. Not only do trout refuse a dragging fly, but they also refuse to take a fly on subsequent casts if they've seen it dragging earlier.

Many main currents in small-stream pools are not central but pushed against one bank of the pool. When that happens, the current still digs the deepest depths right beneath it and still forms the most promising lies in the pool. You'll want to fish up the length of that current tongue, from downstream, but obviously it will have only a single side and center. Fish the inside—that side of the current that spreads into the pool and on which you'll be positioned—first, then fish the center. Run your final drifts right along whatever constricts the far side of the current, whether it's pushed against a low bank, a high bank, or a cliff.

Wherever the main current of a pool butts against a bank or cliff and is turned by it, an eddy, or at least still backwater, will form on the inside of the turn. This will usually be over deep water and is a gathering spot for all sorts of food that falls to the surface of the pool or emerges out of it. It's a prime lie for a trout. It's also a difficult lie to fish without drag. You'll need to lay the line and leader on the water with some slack, or you'll often get drag before trout get a chance to wallop up and take your fly. Sometimes such a lie calls for what is known as a *tower cast* or *pile cast*.

To create this cast, aim your delivery stroke high, to about rod tip height, and underpower it. Then lower your rod until it's just above the water. The line will straighten high in the air, then drop back down toward you and land accordioned on the water. With some practice, you'll be able to set a fly onto the water approximately where you want it, with lots of slack behind it. The current must remove that slack before your fly begins to drag.

When a riffle or run drops into a pool and butts at once against a cliff, it will form an eddy lie on the near side and also set one whirling on the opposite side, across the current from your wading position. This eddy is a prime lie as well, but often a very difficult one to fish.

One of my favorite home streams has just such a lie. The water gathers itself in the tailout of the pool upstream and dashes down a chattering riffle about ten feet long and five feet wide. It enters the pool in a current tongue for just a few feet, then bumps directly into a dark cliff face. Eddies form on both sides before the main current forces its way downstream along the face of the cliff. I have no trouble fishing the main run of the current where it dances, deep and dark, along the face of that cliff. I usually extract at least one trout of some size from the eddy formed at the inside elbow of the pool, where the current turns. But I always have a terrible time taking anything from the eddy on the other side of the current tongue. My fly must fish on the far side of the current, but I have to cast from the near side. It would be easy, except an alder tree clings to the cliff, grows at a tilt, and lowers some branches to within a few feet of the surface of that off-side eddy.

It's one of the few small-stream situations in which I'd like to be carrying a 9-foot rod. The long rod wouldn't be of much use in all the pools I'd fish to get up to that one spot. In that one spot, however, a long rod would let me stand on one side of the current tongue and dap a fly to the other. I'd have to hold the rod low, under those limbs, and it would then be in sight of any trout that might spear up for the fly. But I think I'd catch a trout, because I'd make my movements slowly, and I'd get a good, long drift with my dry fly.

I tried fishing the off-side eddy by dapping over the main current with my short rod a few times, but I got drag before any trout came up. I also tried hanging back, casting across the current, and laying the fly in there with lots of slack behind it. I'd only get a few seconds of free float before the line got tight and whisked the fly out of there. A few times trout rushed it but most of the time they only managed to make splashes right where the fly had been sitting an instant ahead of their arrival. By the time they got there, the fly was gone.

I hooked a trout in the eddy once on a cross-stream cast with lots of slack, placed under that tree and onto the water completely by accident. The trout was a nice one, but it was not hooked well because of all that loose line. It shook the fly. I was never able to execute that same cast without hooking the tree instead of a trout.

I finally took the time, after fishing the pool one day, to stop at the foot of the next pool, turn around, and look at the situation I'd just failed to solve. That's when it entered my head that the current in that small eddy was turned around and headed upstream. The next time I fished the pool, I skipped the off-side eddy, reeled up, hooked the fly into its keeper, and moved up through the riffle to fish the tailout of the next pool. I hooked a small trout, skidded it in and released it. Then I stepped across the riffle, turned to face back downstream, knelt, and shot a cast under the limbs of that tilted tree, onto the eddy I'd never been able to reach. Most of my line landed on rocks at the edge of the eddy. The leader stretched straight to the vortex of the eddy. The fly sat there serenely.

A trout nosed up and took it patiently. It wasn't the largest trout I caught that day, but it was the most satisfying. And it did tell me why I'd never been able to catch a fish from that eddy by setting my fly there from the other side, getting a brief float that I'd always thought was long enough for any small-stream trout to make a decision about, as if I were blaming them for their failure to take my fly fast enough. The dominant trout that lived in that eddy was used to eating things caught in the swirl, unable to fly off in a hurry. The trout came up slowly and took my fly with the same kind of sipping rise a brown accepting crippled mayfly emergers on the Henry's Fork of the Snake River in Idaho might make.

Fly pattern didn't matter there, because the fish was seeing lots of different food forms. But a long float, in terms of time, not distance, did matter.

When casting over any currents that conflict, and cause drag if the fly is delivered on a straight line and leader, you need to use a delivery stroke that installs some slack when the line and leader drop to the water. The easiest way to do this is also the oldest, and you already employ it in your fishing over larger waters. It is the ancient and correct instruction to aim your delivery stroke so that your line straightens in the air two to four feet above the water, rather than as it lands on the water. This waist-high delivery allows the line and leader to relax as they settle to the surface. This slight slack will let the fly float freely, without tug from the leader, on currents that are mildly conflicting.

If the surface currents are tangled enough that you can notice the conflict from where you're casting, you need to add more slack than a relaxed line and leader give. You can get more if you overpower the delivery stroke, so that the line not only straightens in the air above the water but recoils back toward the rod. If you overpower the stroke just a little, the line will straighten and bounce back just enough to add a small amount of slack as the cast drops to the water. If you overpower it a lot, the line will recoil and the cast will settle with lots of slack added.

You can keep control of your cast with some small amount of overpowering. With practice, which in my mind means with lots of fishing, you'll be able to impart some extra muscle to your cast and still get the fly to land where you want it. As you begin overpowering the stroke more and more, the line bounces back less and less predictably, and you lose control of your cast. There are limits to how much extra power you can impart in your delivery stroke without beginning to lose control over where your fly will land. First you'll have to fish enough to get accurate with a straight-line delivery. Then you'll have to decide for yourself how much accuracy you lose with extra power and how much accuracy you're willing to sacrifice to get that slack-line landing and more free drift for your dry fly.

My guess is that you won't want to give up much control over where your fly will go in the restricted spaces that define most small-stream fishing. You'll definitely want to aim your delivery stroke above the water, so your line lands on the water relaxed. You'll also want to learn to overpower your delivery stroke at least a little bit, in order to set your line and leader onto the water with some extra slack. But I doubt you'll gain many extra trout by trying to bounce your cast back toward you. It's a trick worth learning, however, for the times you'll be able to use it in the meadow stream environment, to place flies over rising trout where the currents are confusing.

A more dependable way to get extra slack, when a lot of it is needed to overcome dramatically conflicting currents, is with the wiggle cast. To execute it, you measure some extra line in the air, beyond that required to get the fly to the target. Then you make a delivery stroke that would deliver all of that extra line beyond where you want the fly to land. As the line straightens out toward the lie, wobble the rod tip back and forth briskly. This causes the line and leader to land in a series of S-turns.

The wiggle cast was created to present dry flies downstream to selective trout rising in very smooth currents. That is still its highest and best use. But you'd be surprised how often the addition of just a bit of wiggle to almost any cast will add slack, give the fly a free drift, and fool trout that might have refused your fly without the slack. I often use a tiny bit of wiggle on casts that would not seem to require it, even on small-stream riffles and current tongues fished straight upstream, if I feel I should be taking trout but am not.

Your twin goals, when fishing dry flies over any small-stream water, are to place your fly accurately where you think a trout might be and to get a drag-free drift on that water. About half the time, you'll be able to accomplish both goals—accuracy and a drag-free drift—with a basic cast aimed straight upstream.

The other half of your casts will be creative combinations—curve casts, roll casts, basic casts with wiggle added—that solve specific problems caused by the way water flows in small streams. When you begin creating your own casts to solve your own situations, you're on your swift way toward becoming an expert with dry flies on small waters.

CHAPTER TEN

Dry-Fly Size

WHEN I BEGAN FISHING SMALL STREAMS WITH MY DAD AND BROTHERS, the average dry fly we used was size 10. We had two favorite flies, both big, brushy things. One was called a Beetle Bug and worked out approximately as a local translation of the Royal Wulff. The other was called a Youngs River Special, named after the stream that got logged while I was busy in Southeast Asia. The fly had a deer-hair tail, yellow yarn body, upright and split deer-hair wings, and a collar of brown hackle. It was an approximate Grizzly Wulff, the main differences being the wings and tail, which were bucktail on the more modern Wulff, and the color of the hackle, which on the Wulff would be grizzly.

Another big difference would be the tidiness of the tie and subsequent flotation of the fly. Our deer hair was soft, our body yarns wool, both of which soak up water. Our hackles of the time, imports from India most likely dusted with DDT though we didn't know that then, would not even make the charts today, which begin at the bottom with grade 3. Our hackles might have been grade 5, little better than hen. It took two, sometimes three, of those short feathers to get enough turns of hackle onto the hook to keep the fly afloat for a while.

I know most of you started off with the same fly floatant I did, but I'll tell you about it in case you were lucky enough not to or smart enough to have forgotten. Just before leaving to go fishing, we would take turns in the garage, paring shavings off a block of paraffin, scattering them over a newspaper, folding the newspaper up to funnel the shavings into a Gerber's baby food jar, filling the jar with white gas, twisting the lid down tight. Then all the way to the stream, sitting in the back of the black '52 Chevy sedan, my brothers and I would shake our jars of floatant, checking every few minutes to see if the paraffin had dissolved yet. It was usually ready to float a fly just about the time we got to the stream.

Before casting those size 10 brushpiles that we called Beetle Bugs and Youngs River Specials, we would soak them in this explosive mixture for a few seconds, then remove them, blow on them until we had hyperventilated and were about to pass out. Before fishing them we'd set them onto the water in the side shallows, where no trout would be able to see them, and let some of the gas wick off. The first cast or two would always cause pretty little oil slicks.

It's no great surprise that trout would rush those oversize dry flies and either strike them with a wallop intended to inflict fatal damage or take a horrified look and flee from them. Our main dry-fly tactic in those days was to fish a Beetle Bug upstream to the current tongues and over the deepest parts of all the pools we came across as we rock-hopped and scrambled upstream. Our main backup strategy, if that failed, was to change to the Youngs River Special and fish it upstream to the same places, in the same ways.

If both flies failed, then the day became categorized as one that fell into the unfortunate part of our early philosophy that trout on small streams would take dry flies or nothing at all. Strangely, in those days before that stream got logged, days of failure were fairly rare. A couple of things likely contributed to that. First, the watershed was in the maturity of its second growth, recovered from the first logging at the turn of the century, and quite healthy. The stream was full of hungry trout. Second, it was seldom fished, at least in the parts where we fished it.

The reason for that was simple enough. The first logging was all done by rail. The tracks were laid up the entire length of the stream, on the first level bench above its narrow floodplain. Equipment was delivered for the logging operation, and logs were extracted out of the watershed, all on trains. After the ancient old-growth forest was flattened and freighted from the watershed during that first logging, the rails were dismantled, hauled to the next watershed, and set up for the logging of that one.

All that remained of the railroad, when I first fished the stream a half century after that first logging, was the compacted soil of its bed and in some places the remnants of rotted crossties. The timberwork of a few trestles, left standing over tributary canyons, still stood among the trees that had by then grown up all around them. These trestles were gone to rot, covered with moss, truly beautiful remains of a time not long past.

The railroad bed that we hiked alongside the stream, through the deep second-growth timber, was covered by moss, grown to ferns and carpets of candyflowers. But the soil, compacted by the passing of thousands of weighted trains, was apparently not soft enough for softwoods and hardwoods to take root. Successive generations of deer, elk, and bears found the abandoned railroad bed the line of least resistance on their travels up and down the watershed. So the roadbed remained an open woodland trail as the watershed grew toward second-growth maturity: a tunnel through the trees on a bench just above the stream.

This trail followed the stream several miles away from a new logging road that crossed it far upstream and another that crossed it far downstream. Where we went, and saw so few folks, was in all those miles between the roads. Trout in the pools in that long stretch of stream rarely saw flies and were usually willing to accept our big and awful ones.

It took a long time, though not forever, to discover that cutting the size of the flies back a bit increased the number of trout that were willing to take them solidly and decreased the number of days when the trout, as we then thought, would take nothing at all. My standard fly patterns did not change much for many years, though I used the local favorites less and less and tied the look-alike Royal and Grizzly Wulffs more and more.

Through the middle years of my small-stream fishing life, my standard tie was a size 12 dressing. Except for Parachute Hoppers and Stimulators, both of which imitate insects that are often size 10 or even 8, that's the largest size dry fly in my small-stream box today. My first fly out of the box, on an average day astream, even on a remote wilderness stream, will now be a size 14. If you were to hold a brushy size 10 dry fly in the palm of your hand and place next to it a more moderately tied size 14, you would see that the 14 is not just a couple of sizes smaller: It gives the appearance of an insect about one third to one-half the overall size of the 10.

Reducing the size of the dry flies fished on small streams—from size 10 and sometimes 12, in those early days tied to excess, down to a maximum size 12, more often size 14, sometimes size 16, all tied to full but not expanded proportions—made a big difference in my small-stream dry-fly fishing, and it will in yours as well. Part of this diminution in size was prompted by the availability of better materials with which to tie the flies: domestic hackles, better deer and yearling elk hairs, water repellent furs and synthetics in place of wool yarns. Another part was propelled by my awakening to the knowledge that a boil under a fly was not a sign of hesitant approval, but a sign of absolute, if last-second, rejection: That trout would never be back, though another, most often smaller, might take the fly and make me think it was the first.

A final push toward reduction in dry-fly size came from observation of the natural insects along trout streams. Most mayflies are sizes 14 and 16, some smaller, though you'll see an occasional green drake lifting off, so big it makes you want to duck out of its way. Most caddis are sizes 12 and 14, though many small streams have hatches of fall caddis that take wing at size 8 and up. The most abundant stoneflies, notably olive and yellow sallies, run to size 16 and sometimes even smaller, though widespread and prolific golden stones are exceptions that should be accounted for with big Stimulators in your fly box.

If you reduce the size of your dry flies you fish on small streams to bring them into line with the average-size insects trout eat there, you might be surprised at the sudden jump in your success. Most of this will be because trout are more confident about eating things that are the same size as what they've been eating all day, all their lives. No small part of the increase in your success will be due to the requirement that you move in closer and fish at shorter range, in order to follow the float of those smaller flies, to notice when trout take them. This closeness causes you to be cautious in your approach to the water and also allows you a more accurate read of the water and a more accurate placement of your fly upon it.

Learning to approach as close as you can, thereby being able to fish as short as you can without alerting trout to your presence and rendering them impossible to catch, is just as important as carrying the right set of flies for small streams and learning the right set of casts with which to present them.

CHAPTER ELEVEN

Nymph Tactics

My introduction to nymphing on small streams was about as comical as my attempts to fish them with overlong leaders. The reasons were also about the same. I'd been reading in outdoor magazines of the times that the way to fish nymphs was to tie them weighted; rig to fish them the same as you would dry flies, on 10- to 12-foot leaders; cast them upstream; fish them back down toward you; watch the line tip for any jump or twitch. That sounded simple. I rushed out to try it.

I caught few trout.

It's likely I got lots of takes. I cast up into rough current tongues, watched the line tip as the fly sank and drifted toward me. I didn't get the news about many of those hits. It was difficult to notice any unusual movement of the line tip in water that bounced. If I ever did notice it, the trout that caused it had almost always spit the fly and run before I set the hook. The fly would blow over my head and get stuck in the trees behind me. It was a lot like my early dry-fly fishing but without the fish.

I caught an occasional trout by accident, usually while lifting the line for the next cast and discovering a trout was already attached to the fly and probably had been for its entire drift. If the trout had any size, I'd set against it, play it out in panic, and sometimes bring it to hand. If it was tiny, I'd often launch it into a backcast. There is little more distressing, in small-stream fly fishing, than an innocent subsize trout flapping about on land, a fly in its mouth, its life expiring. I was almost always able to rescue them, but I was not able to rescue my enthusiasm for fishing nymphs rigged as I would dry flies.

My next attempts were almost as frustrating. They were inspired by magazine articles about advanced nymphing: rigging with a strike indicator on the upper end of the leader and split shot at the lower end, just a foot or so above the nymph. The standard formula called for placement of the indicator twice the depth of the water above the fly. So I fished with my indicator, a hard one of cork painted fluorescent orange, about four to six feet up the leader from the fly. A couple of split shot, in hindsight clearly oversize for the water I was on, were pinched onto the leader at its opposite end.

I caught nothing but the bottom.

It didn't take many attempts at these sorts of literature-inspired nymphing tactics to drive me back to my old philosophy that if small-stream trout would not take dry flies, they would not take anything else either. I suspected that was not true, but I hung my hat on it for many of my youthful years because my attempts to fish anything but dry flies caught far more troubles than trout. It's my guess that the same frustration caused my small-stream mentors to develop that original theory about dry flies or nothing that they passed down to me as a small-stream fact.

One day I went driving and exploring far into the headwater basin of a stream I'd fished almost all of my life. I was, in truth, not looking for fishing but scouting for a wild blackberry patch in an old logging cut, when I crossed the beginnings of the stream on a wooden bridge. The water was tiny way up there. A pool just downstream from the bridge looked miniature but pretty. A chattery riffle entered the pool and formed a current tongue. This bent around a gravel bar on the inside and pushed against a gray sandstone bank on the outside. The depths of the pool, no more than two feet, were right where the current tongue got redirected by the high bank.

It was midsummer. I had the customary fly rod and belt bag in the rig, along with berry buckets. I'd been on a trip to Arizona not long before to fish the Lees Ferry stretch of the Colorado River, about as far as you can get from a small stream. Oversize fans of yellow yarn, as sensitive strike indicators that revealed every touch a trout might make to a nymph drifting along beneath them, had been pioneered on that water not long before I got there. I had some outsize luck fishing with those fans of yarn on the Colorado. One trout I caught weighed more than seven pounds. When I got home, I knotted a hank of the yellow yarn to a D-ring on the outside of my belt bag, awaiting future opportunities to try the new technique on old waters.

I did not expect to catch trout of any size so far up one of my old home streams, but I decided to see what might be in that pretty pool. That yarn indicator material, brought back from Arizona, caught my eye when I sat to rig up on the gravel bar alongside the pool downstream from the bridge. I decided, without any reasoning to my thinking, to try it. I rigged with a weighted A. P. Black nymph, size 12, and a small fan of yellow yarn to suspend it. I glanced at the water, forgot the correct calculations for depth, and slip-knotted the yarn into the leader just a couple of feet above the fly. I teased the yarn into the appropriate fan shape, then dressed it with floatant, just as I would a dry fly.

I did not stand up from my seat on the gravel bar to deliver my first cast with that simple nymph rig. I merely stripped a few feet of line from the reel, drew it out beyond the rod tip, held the hook while I danced a bit of line into the air above the gravel, like a snake charmer elevates a cobra, then flicked the rod toward the upstream end of the pool and let the fly go at the same time. The fly shot out, pipped into the water just upstream from the deepest spot in the pool. The indicator landed behind it, lay on its side a moment while the fly sank, and erected itself when the fly tugged at it.

No more than a foot of drift later the indicator darted under when something tugged at the nymph. I hoisted the trout out, landed it thrashing in my lap, subdued and unhooked it, admired it a moment before tossing it back into the dark water from which it had been flown. It was a native cutt, black on the back, silver on the belly, finely spotted on its sides, crimson slashed at its throat. It was fully nine inches long, a monster for the water in which it lived.

I fished an hour up that tiny stream, extracted trout on the nymph and indicator rig from almost every pool. The size of the first one I'd caught, I discovered, was the rule rather than the exception.

Success on small streams, fishing that abbreviated nymph rig, became a rule as well. I do it quite often now, and I resort to nymphs fairly quickly if trout refuse drys. At times, when conditions seem all wrong for dry flies, I rig a nymph and fish it first.

Conditions that seem right for nymphs, therefore wrong for drys, include cool or cold water, a lack of insects in the air or on the water to get trout looking up, any color in the water to impede the sight of trout as they watch for food, or an air temperature that is substantially cool for the season or compared with the water temperature. In the presence of just one or two of these factors, I still might try a dry. When the factors begin to add up, however, I jump right to a nymph. I'll give you an example.

It happened in south Wisconsin, on a small spring creek that ran through pastureland. Cattle had cropped the grass almost to the edges, leaving tufts and rows of it right at the waterline in places where the banks were too steep for fat dairy cows to descend safely. It was a pretty little pastoral stream, but it suffered from an excess of nutrition on account of cow crap. It was just a bit off-color when I fished it.

I fished this stream early one summer morning, before aquatic insects had awakened and begun to hatch, and before the sun had a chance to bake the previous night's moisture out of the earth, warm up terrestrial insects, and prod them into taking chances near water. The air was still cooler than the water, though later in the day the air would be much warmer and change all the equations. I would fish drys then, matching a hatch if it happened, hoppers if nothing else was indicated. Meanwhile, I desired some action, and a nymph seemed the most likely thing to provide it. I rigged almost exactly as I had on the headwaters of that tiny home headwater stream, but the spring creek was deeper, so I fixed the small fan of yellow yarn four feet up from my fly.

The fly was an Olive Beadhead nymph, size 14, which was not an accidental choice. On account of its stable flows and excess of enrichment, the stream had an abundance of rooted weed beds. A few kick net samples had revealed these weeds to be squirming with scuds. These small crustaceans survive by a simple law of nature: They are the color of the background on which they live, or they stand out and get eaten. They were olive.

I selected the beadhead rather than an imitative scud dressing because the weight of the bead would cause it to sink, but not very fast and not very far. I wanted it to get a foot or a little more than that deep. I didn't want it to get into constant quarrels with the weeds above which I wanted it to fish. I also selected it because beadhead nymphs work wonders on small waters.

The stream was narrow, seven to eight feet wide at its widest, usually narrower than that. Most of its holding lies were current sweeps along the banks, where the stream dug under the edges. It was beautiful water, if you were able to look past its slight lack of clarity, with lots of bends that formed undercuts on their outsides, beneath those grassy banks.

It was not unlike the Wisconsin spring creek I'd fished not far away, with a dry fly, between tall walls of grass. The difference was the cattle, which kept the grass from growing head-high, though they also kept the water from clearing up. Take away the cows and this one would become that one in a season of growth for its grass.

Because of its almost vertical banks, the only way to fish this creek was to insert myself into it, wade right up it. I slid down there, unhooked my beadhead from its keeper, and began to fish it with short upstream casts right along the edges. The trout were browns. They came from all the likely lies along the banks. They were plump on good feed. It was fun to watch the yellow indicator settle into a drift inches from a bank, bobbing brightly along on dark and cloudy currents, then suddenly twitching, stopping, or even diving under.

It was challenging casting. If the beadhead drifted more than a foot out from the bank, the cast was wasted. If the beadhead landed on the bank and hung up in the grass, the line of lies downstream from it was wasted, because I'd have to wade up and unhook it. Wisconsin grass is tough. If the cast landed so close to the grass that the fly and indicator skirted the edge by less than six inches, action was almost certain to happen.

The yarn rig, suspending either a weighted nymph or a beadhead, became my standard for nymphing small streams. I tried hard indicators, which support more weight, but did not find that ability necessary for the size nymphs I like to fish, primarily 12s and 14s, sometimes 16s, on small streams. I also did not enjoy the more splashy landing hard indicators make and the way they show themselves unnaturally on the water. A little fluff of yellow yarn looks like it has some chance to be an insect, though trout rarely mistake it for one. But they seem less put off by the yarn drifting so near the nymph than they do by a bright bit of painted cork or foam. That might all be my imagination, but if I imagine it, then it becomes real in my fishing.

Perhaps I prefer yarn indicators because I tried them first on small streams, and they caught fish for me. On rough water of central current tongues, more buoyant hard indicators float more dependably and are easier to see, so they might work better there than yarn. On softer side currents, where trout often hang out waiting for terrestrial insects to drop in, yarn indicators are less obtrusive and help fool more fish. I am not willing to switch indicators as I move from one piece of holding water to the next, so I stick with yarn indicators on small streams.

The indicator should be fixed on the leader high enough to show the dangling nymph to trout holding along the bottom. I no longer subscribe to the old rule for placing the indicator twice the depth of the water up the leader. That does work, as a reference point, on bigger water. On small streams, it often lets the fly sink and take root on the bottom, rather than drift. Such distant placement always removes the indicator farther from the fly than I like, because it lengthens the transmission line that relays information about what happens to the nymph down below to the drifting indicator up above. I start with the indicator the depth of the water above the fly, and move it higher if I'm getting fewer hits than I think the bit of water I'm fishing should provide.

I fish this simple nymph and indicator outfit almost exactly as I would a dry fly in the same situation. I work upstream and fish all the likely lies at the tailout, along the length of the current tongue, and the corner pockets of the average small-stream pool. If likely lies, signs of trout, or other indications make me think that the shallower, slower water along the edges of the pool might be productive, then I set the fly and indicator rig there and let it ride out a long, slow drift on those placid currents. As I move from pool to pool, I cast the same rig to any bench or pocket lies that look deep enough to hold trout.

If there is a difference in the way I fish this nymph rig as opposed to a dry fly on the same water, it's that I try to be more watchful of both the strike indicator and things that might affect what I'm doing. It's easier to notice a take to a dry than it is to a nymph beneath an indicator, unless the strike pulls the indicator directly under. Just as often, it's a hesitation in the drift or a mere twitch of the yarn. If the nymph hangs the bottom too often, it's necessary to shorten the distance between the fly and the indicator. If it never touches bottom and trout never touch it, then it's wise to increase the distance between nymph and indicator.

Though it's wise to do it, I do not often adjust the position of my indicator up and down the leader as I move from one piece of water to the next. Because water depth changes constantly as you move up a small stream, in theory it's best to change the depth your nymph will fish just as constantly. In practice, in the restricted environment of a small stream, you'd be required to move your indicator after almost every cast. I try to average out the depth of the stream I'm fishing, and fish without minor adjustments as I move along. I recommend you do the same if you rig as I do, with a hank of yarn slip-knotted into your leader. It's not an easy rig to adjust. Hard indicators held on with tooth-picks are easier to adjust, another factor in their favor. You might like them better than I do, and by now you should have the idea to at least try them.

In the end, I usually wind up with my strike indicator and nymph separated by just a few inches more than the average depth of the stream I'm fishing. That shows the fly drifting along, just above the bottom, in easy sight and striking range of most trout holding down there, without getting hung up very often.

I'm not the most ambitious angler around when it comes to rigging and constant rerigging. I don't enjoy snagging bottom, losing a setup, then patiently rebuilding it again, only to cast it out and risk losing it again. This defect in my character removes me from any chance to make the list of top nymphers, even in a small group. Rick Hafele, with whom I cowrote *Western Hatches* twenty years ago, rigs first with nymphs unless indications for something else are overwhelming. He is deadly with them. If one of us vastly outfishes the other, does the kind of destruction that is hard even on an ego that never bothers to count trout, it will be Rick outdoing me nine times out of ten, and always when he is nymphing and I am not.

Rick doesn't mind losing flies, if in the trade he can catch a few more trout. I do. So I was surprised that Rick introduced me to an excellent way to show a nymph to trout without taking much chance of losing it. He did not invent the method, but he got to it before I did, and I'm glad he revealed it to me rather than conceal it from me, as he often does with other aspects of his success whenever he can get away with it. But he did try.

We fished the small stream on which he did the research for his mas-ter's degree in aquatic entomology. The day was typical for the Oregon coast, even in summer, with a light and low cloud cover that produced a fine drizzle most of the morning. Sun would burn it off later, and things would look different, but we'd camped alongside the stream and didn't want to wait around for trout to get happy about dry flies. It seemed a sacrilege to start with anything else, even to Rick, so we tied on what we knew would work later in the day, size 12 Elk Hairs. They failed.

After a short time, I switched to a drab version of the same beast, a Deer Hair Caddis with an olive body and gray wing. Usually that change is enough to enliven at least a few fish, but going to the darker fly didn't brighten my prospects that morning. Rick fiddled with his rigging about the same time I did, but he took a position that kept his back to me while he did. I assumed he was rerigging to fish a nymph and indicator and was not far wrong.

We skipped pools that day, each of us fishing every other one. Leapfrogging doesn't work where the stream is so restricted that thrashing past would ruin the other person's fishing. So I stopped to watch idly, not long after we'd both made our changes, while Rick probed a nice pool that started out in the drop of a minor waterfall, spread out in a froth of uprising bubbles, then darkened over minor depths. Rick shot his dry fly right to the end of the froth, the beginning of the deep water. He had not, it appeared to me, even bothered to change flies. He still had on the bright-winged Elk Hair Caddis.

We both watched it float. I was taken aback when it suddenly disappeared from the surface. Rick was not. He shouted and set the hook. The Elk Hair Caddis came quivering and dancing out of the water on a line taut to something beneath it. I needn't go on with the story. You know that Rick had dangled a nymph on a couple feet of tippet, tied to the hook bend of the same dry he'd been using when he was catching the same thing I was: nothing.

That was quite a few years ago. A nymph dropped beneath a dry fly has become standard procedure for exploring small streams, and any other streams for that matter, when indications are not specific for any particular fly type. The combination of a dry and a nymph offers trout a choice. Some days they'll take only the nymph, in which case it's smart to nip the dry out of the leader, replace it with a yarn indicator, though Rick would say a hard indicator. Either way, you're a lot less likely to get hooked on an indicator than you are to get barbed by a dry fly. Some days they'll refuse the nymph but willingly take the dry fly. In that case, cut off the nymph. It's difficult to release a squirming trout with an extra hook flying around. If you don't get caught by it, the trout you've just unpinned from the dry might get repinned by the nymph, causing extra troubles.

If you're taking some trout on the dry, others on the nymph, then that's the perfect equation, and you should leave both flies on your leader. There's another good reason to let both the dry fly and nymph continue to fish, even when the proportion of catch falls more to one than the other: If the balance is not entirely one way or the other, continuing to fish both flies lets you know when trout change their minds.

They might suddenly refuse the dry and take only the nymph, or the opposite, take the nymph and disdain the dry. Either way, if you're fishing both, you'll know it happened. If you're fishing one or the other, all you'll know is that you stopped catching fish. You won't have any concrete evidence that tells you what to do about it.

I mentioned that I fish nymphs with yarn indicators pretty much the same way I fish dry flies on the same water. Dry and nymph dropper combinations are fished the same way you'd fish the dry by itself on the same set of currents. I won't get into advice here. Just drop the nymph off the stern of the dry fly and continue to fish as if it were not even there.

Rigging requires some mild sense, no more. First, make sure the leader to your dry fly is one that is easy to control on the water where you're casting. If it's too long, or at the edge of being difficult to turn over and cast with accuracy, cut it back a bit and rework the tippet so it's in balance with the size dry you're going to use to suspend a nymph. A rough rule for the size of the dry is one hook size larger than the nymph you plan to drop beneath it. For me, this most often dictates a size 12 dry over a size 14 nymph, but almost as often a size 14 dry over a size 16 nymph.

I rarely use a size 10 dry to suspend a size 12 nymph, because I consider both of those on the high side of what I expect trout to be eager to accept. A size 10 dry might fool sufficient small-stream trout to keep you happy. But you should watch the water carefully for those slight boils and bulges that are signs a trout has rushed the fly but then turned away and refused it. If you get those, it's likely you're getting them from the very trout you'd most like to catch: the largest ones.

If you are catching nothing but small trout, drop to a smaller size fly and see if it makes a difference. I have no problem with size 12 nymphs on small streams; trout seem to take them well. But they're difficult to suspend beneath anything smaller than size 10 drys, and I feel that a dry that large reduces my chances to take trout unless stoneflies are in the air or hoppers are in the grasses. In that case, I like those large drys and drop whatever size nymph I want from their hook bends.

The nymph should be at least one size smaller than the dry fly, not because that size is more likely to be taken by trout, but because it is more likely to let the dry fly remain afloat. The tippet you tie to the nymph should be one size finer than the tippet to the dry, not because it needs to be finer to fool fish but because you want it to break first if the nymph gets hung up. Maybe this strikes back to my laziness about rerigging, but I can't see a reason to lose two flies and the tippet between them when you can lose just one fly and no tippet and get rerigged quickly.

The nymph tippet should be 18 inches to 2 feet long, as a rough rule, for control of the cast rather than to get the nymph to any specific depth. The idea is to get the nymph through the surface film and fishing a few inches deep, not to sink it to the bottom. If you want to fish the bottom, rig with the standard split shot and strike indicator setup. When you fish a nymph as a dropper beneath a dry fly, keep the tippet to the nymph short enough that you can cast without the nymph flipping around and getting into tangles with the dry or with streamside vegetation. Three feet of tippet to the nymph is about the longest I use on small water.

Use the improved clinch knot to fix the tippet to the bend of the dry fly. The result is a simple rig, not unlike the nymph rig with a yarn strike indicator, but one that offers the trout an option: dry or nymph.

The dry and dropper rig is my favorite for exploring new water or for fishing old water on days when I don't know what kind of fly trout will prefer. Specifically, given no indications that I should do something different, I'll rig a 7½-foot 4X leader to a size 12 Deer Hair Caddis, add 2 feet of 5X tippet, and drop a size 14 Olive Beadhead.

This has become my standard exploring rig, in part because the two flies—the drab caddis-shaped dry and the Olive Beadhead nymph—look like so many of the abundant food forms trout feed on constantly in small streams. But it has become my favorite rig in larger part because I've used it often, on so many waters all across the continent, and caught lots of trout on it.

One of my most memorable small-stream trout came on this combination, in a mountain hollow high up in the Appalachian Mountains. I'd been invited to speak at a regional conclave sponsored by the Trout Unlimited chapter in Hickory, North Carolina, one early May. The day after the conclave James Fortner and Carl Freeman drove me to a stream they were wise enough not to name, though they were kind enough not to blindfold me. It was a pretty place, in a mountainous oak forest with a laurel understory. The stream was steep. The water tumbled over and among large granite boulders, formed pools that were short but deep. The water was very clean and clear. Streambed stones were bare and entirely without silt, a surprise to somebody who has grown up in logging country and became used to slipping and sliding up degraded waters that had once been pristine.

I'd been given a choice before we went up into the mountains to fish that stream. One option was to fish private property in the lowlands, on a stream that started up in the mountains but got placid by the time it entered the property. It was heavily stocked with brown trout. I had been taken out to it the day before, watched while the owner sprinkled the trout's evening meal over it. The water erupted with splashes and boils of almost frightening size. Perhaps I was afraid to fish it. The second choice was the small mountain stream. I was told to expect ten-inch rainbows and browns, none native, but all wild. That sounded fine to me, though I'd have been more pleased to catch the native brookies that had been displaced.

It was quite a hike getting down to the water, on an old grade cut at a descent across the face of a hillside, through the laurel and oak. We came across a lean-to shelter that had not been used in a decade or so, overgrown by creepers and moss. I asked James, who's in real estate, and Carl, who's in insurance, to stand next to it, hands extended to present it, as if showing it to a would-be buyer. I take such photos wherever I go, to show my wife when I get home and tell her I liked where I was so much that I bought a place for us to move there.

I liked where I was on that North Carolina trout stream.

We hit the stream and fished from ten in the morning until about two in the afternoon, then stopped for lunch. The water was reminiscent of my home streams before they got logged. The three of us sat atop a giant boulder, eating sandwiches, looking downstream at water we'd already rock-hopped and waded up through, and looking upstream at water we still had ahead of us, dropping steeply out of the laurel and oak forest. What astonished me most was the contrast between my perceptions of North Carolina trout streams and the reality on which I was fishing.

My vision was of lowland streams meandering through sycamore forests, full of fallen limbs, swampy and dark at the edges, absent of trout, full of snakes. That was not entirely based on wild guesses. I went through infantry officer candidate school in the late 1960s at Fort Benning, Georgia. We spent a lot of time out in the boonies. We waded streams just like I described, mostly at night. Of course, they were not trout streams. And they were not full of snakes. But a fellow in a platoon that followed mine had a cottonmouth swim up to him under the water and bite him in the leg. That was Georgia, not North Carolina.

The reality, much higher up in those Appalachian Mountains, was pleasant. The water was as clear as any I'd ever seen anywhere. What surprised me most was leaping from rock to rock, wearing felted brogues, and sticking when I landed. The bottoms of my home streams are all at least slightly silted from past loggings. Most desert streams I've fished in the West are somewhat silted from overgrazing. The abundance of Rocky Mountain streams I've fished usually have thin coats of photosynthetic growth on bottom rocks, from all that sunshine they get.

Streambed boulders and stones in that North Carolina stream were as clean as if laundered. Because they were granitic, their surfaces were rough. My felts adhered to them. It took me a while to adjust to that. I'd gotten so used to slipping, over all the years I've fished small streams, that at times I threw myself off balance when I leaped and landed and stuck.

The trout we'd caught before lunch, which were many, were what I'd been promised: ten-inch rainbows and browns. Some were larger, but just a bit. Most were smaller, but not by much. I was satisfied with that, pleased by the day, happy I'd gotten the opportunity to fish such a beautiful stream in a setting that surprised me.

A modest hatch of fairly large and faintly olive mayfly duns began while we ate. I captured one in a small aquarium net I always carry and examined it. It was clearly from a clinging nymph; its head retained the flattened shape of the head of the nymph. That made sense, given the fast water and siltless streambed. Clingers do best in riffles and rapids of clean streams. I didn't have enough experience with eastern hatches to fit this bug into the taxonomic scheme of things. I didn't have anything, in the single small fly box I carried, to match it. I've corrected that by adding René Harrop's Olive Hairwing Dun in sizes 12 to 16. It covers a wide range of hatches that happen on small streams and on all others. It floats well and is easy to see on the water. But I added that dressing to my list of small-stream flies as a result of the hatch that happened that day in North Carolina, which means I had none of them when I needed them.

Nevertheless, I had no trouble finding and tying on a dry fly that I thought matched the natural fairly well, a size 12 Deer Hair Caddis. Strangely, when we descended from our rock and began fishing upstream again, we saw no rises to the duns and got few rises to the drys we'd all tied on to represent them. This made me suspect trout were too busy taking the nymphs down below to bother about the duns on the surface. When I reached the tailout of a long pool that was deep in relation to the water I'd been fishing, four feet or so, I stopped, searched my fly box, arrived at an Olive Beadhead nymph in size 14, and dropped it from the stern of the caddis pattern on 2 feet of 5X tippet.

I fished the tailout and caught nothing, which puzzled me because it looked more productive than a lot of water I'd caught trout out of earlier. I made my first cast to the body of the pool, all of about twenty-five feet, up to that spot I've described so carefully and now probably too often: where the current tongue loses most of its force and spreads out over the deepest water in the pool. The dry fly floated two or three feet, then popped under. I lifted the rod to set the hook. It's a good thing I was fishing Skip Morris's rod with that touch of softness in its tip.

From the second of the set, it was clear a lot of weight was out there. A shout of surprise got goosed out of me. James and Carl reeled up, rushed up from the pools they'd been fishing downstream, and watched my antics as I tried to keep from losing that trout. It lofted out of the water once. It was so outsize for the pool it was in that we didn't even ooh or aah about it. It came down from the jump awkwardly on that fragile 5X but didn't break it.

The trout could easily have made a run straight upstream or down, gone out of that pool and into the next. I'd not have been able to do anything about it and would not have been able to follow it far. This trout, like most big ones, was reluctant to leave its territory. It must have worked a long time to establish its station and then its size, tucking into those ten-inchers we'd been catching all day.

It was a brown. I cradled its belly in one palm, and the trout sagged over my hand at both ends. I held it underwater, lifted it for a quick photo, lowered it and restrained it by the tail. James looked at it, said, "I've fished this stream for twenty years and I've never caught a trout from it that weighed more than two pounds."

Carl said, "It must weigh six."

I guessed it at no more than five but kept quiet about that. In all the years I spent flying around speaking to fishing clubs at conclaves and sportsmens shows—I retired young, just last year, from the hecticness of that—it's the only time that going out fishing afterward enhanced my reputation. But I know as well as you do that catching that big trout was entirely an accident.

It's no accident that my favorite exploring rig for small streams, quickly after that trip and so far forever after, became a size 14 Olive

Beadhead nymph dropped two feet off the tail end of a size 12 Deer Hair Caddis.

I sometimes use a large and heavily weighted nymph to probe deep pockets in fast water and also to plunge right down into the abrupt depths of mountain pools that are formed by miniature waterfalls. Usually the nymph is Charlie Brooks's Montana Stone, in size 8 or 10. It's a portly thing that is big, black, and ugly, fattened by twenty to thirty wraps of lead wire on the hook shank. It hits the water with a thump and plummets down like a stone. Most of the time I rig it with no indicator. If I use an indicator, it will be a giant fan of the same yellow yarn I usually use in smaller amounts, to suspend less weighty nymphs.

In cascades studded with boulders that break the flow and create brief holding lies for trout, the best way to fish a heavy nymph is to get right up onto the lie, within ten to at most twenty feet. Cast two to five feet upstream from the obstruction that forms the potential lie. Give the nymph time to sink on a slack line and leader. Then lift your rod high and escort the fly as it tumbles through the water that you suspect might hold trout. Watch for signs of a take: the leader suddenly straightening, the line tip darting, a flash or wink underwater, the indicator, if you're using one, moving contrary to the current. You might even feel a hit.

Be patient. Make several casts. Things will happen differently down there on every cast. Sometimes the shifting currents will lift the fly. Sometimes they will open up and let the fly fall right to the bottom. Give the trout every chance to see the fly in a way that makes them want to take it.

To fish a plunge pool, take a position right up next to the head, where the water from upstream dives in. Flip that heavy fly into the downward flow itself—the waterfall, if there is one—so that it is driven to the bottom by the force of the same current that carves the depths right at the top end of the pool. Let the fly sink a moment or so, then lift your rod and escort the fly along as it is delivered downstream, you hope at the bottom. Again, repeat the cast often because currents will do different things to the fly on every drift.

Be sure to show the nymph near enough to any soft corners that trout holding there will notice it drifting past them. They'll dart into the flow to take it. They're used to doing that; that's why they're there; that's how they make a living.

I've seen a fast-water nymphing tactic applied in California that looks valuable, but I've not been able to make it work in my own fishing, mostly because I haven't tried it enough to learn it well. It's one of those local tactics, worked out on specific waters, that work where they're devised, and work on waters that are similar anywhere in the world, but that take a lot of time to learn to execute correctly. I don't fish the kinds of waters where this one works often enough to have done that. If you fish waters shaped for it, you should learn it.

The water where I watched it work is the North Pitt, a Sierra stream that bounds west down the mountains, pauses at a power impoundment, and bounds down some more. After it leaves the impoundment, its flows are no longer natural, so it lacks the normal pushing back of its banks. Fishing is good when the power is on, but the flow is heavy and constricted for the size streambed down which it dashes. The stream is small but brutal to wade against. It is very difficult to fish. It's a leg-breaker.

Trout lies are along the bottom, two to four feet deep, where the swift water is interrupted by boulders from basketball to beachball size. While I was there no hatches happened, and trout had no incentive to feed on the surface. I was with an expert on the stream, Pete Giampaoli of Chico, California. He said it's rare to fish the North Pitt with anything but nymphs. It quickly became obvious to me that Pete knew precisely what he was talking about.

I was one-armed at the time, had a shoulder already scheduled for surgery. As soon as I saw the water, after we'd descended into its canyon below the dam, I decided I'd use my one good limb for the wading staff, forget fishing, watch Pete. I think I'd have caught about the same number of trout had I done the opposite: forgotten the staff, concentrated on fishing.

Pete is midheight, not heavy, but firmly built and a strong wader. You would be that or you would not like that water. He used no staff but eased himself along very slowly, sort of flowing upstream against the flow of the water rushing downstream, inserting himself into eddies behind protruding boulders, which were, by the way, a part of the beauty of that very beautiful stream. Because the stream was protected from spate by the dam, the boulders had tall tufts of grass, ferns, and patches of yellow monkey flowers rooted and growing on top. So picture it: deep, fast, and clear currents braiding around granite boulders that stand out like little islands in the stream. It was pretty, but it wasn't productive water for me.

Pete rigged with a heavily weighted nymph, I don't know what pattern, but we'll call it generic, something like a Gold Ribbed Hare's Ear, around size 12. The A. P. Black would have done well, but I tie it for small streams with only about eight to ten turns of lead wire. For Pete's water, it would need fifteen to twenty turns and might still need a split shot or two pinched to the leader. Pete's leader, if I recall it correctly, was a sort of ladder, with the nymph at the end, a single shot six or so inches from the fly, and another the same number of inches above that.

About a foot and a half or two above the fly, he molded a bright indicator of putty and added another a foot above that. Pete then waded within rod reach of the line of current he wanted to fish. He cast to the upstream end of a line of lies, let all his rigging sink, then high-sticked the outfit, following the drift of the fly along the bottom. He watched the progress of the two strike indicators submerged in the clear water. The trick, as Pete explained it to me, is to notice any unusual movement of the indicators as they drift in parallel down the current.

He repeated the cast over and over. All trout got lots of chances to get a whack at Pete's nymph. It was fun to watch him work, and I'll back away for a bit of advice that is good for any water you fish, small or large, and any species you might fish for, trout or not: If you're with somebody who knows a method you don't, don't focus on your own fishing, perhaps to try to outfish him. Instead, sheath your rod and watch him closely. Learn all you can. Apply it later, as soon as you get a chance.

After watching Pete awhile, I made an effort to catch trout with a standard nymph rig: a weighted nymph, two split shot eight inches above it, and a buoyant strike indicator twice the depth of the water up the leader. I leaned on my staff and tried to fish with my wounded wing. I hooked one trout.

Pete caught ten in the two hours we fished. The surgery was successful. I haven't been back to California for fishing since and don't find that kind of water—a small stream interrupted by a dam and then continuing its dash—very often in my travels.

It's a nymphing method that could be applied, perhaps with less weight, on many other streams. The water needs to be clear so those indicators can be watched while they're submerged. The flow needs to be fast, the depth somewhat consistent, the lies among boulders along the bottom. Given those conditions on a small stream, I still suspect you and I would need quite a bit of time to master the method. I'm sure it took time for Pete to master it as well.

Part of it is personality. Pete is a strong, aggressive wader. It was easy to see he was at home in the bounce and boil of the North Pitt. I would never do as well as he would there, given two good shoulders and all the time I ever wanted to practice his nymphing method. I'd wind up sitting dazed on one of those boulders, taking in the beauty of the stream. Then I'd go off looking for gentler waters, more suited to the way I want to fish.

But I did learn from Pete and applied what I learned from him on waters that I fish most often. When nymphing fast water now, I tend to do it with my old and simple rig, a yellow fan of yarn supporting a mildly weighted nymph. But I often add a split shot or two to the leader, inches from the fly. And I edge right up alongside the current tongue or run of water I want to fish, stoop or kneel next to it, and high-stick my nymph right down the current slot in front of me. Getting up close gives me more control of the drift and puts me in position to notice more subtle shifts in the posture of the indicator.

I hook more trout. And it reminds me of the single-egg fishing I did as a kid: edging up to a current tongue, flicking a bait of eggs upstream, holding my rod high as it drifted along the bottom in front of me, setting the hook at any hesitation in the progress of the leader. That's nostalgic. It's interesting the way we add a tactic to our small-stream repertoire midway through a fly-fishing life, only to recall that it's almost what we did when we began.

CHAPTER TWELVE

Working Wet Flies

IN THE LATE 1980S I DEVELOPED A LARGE DESIRE TO TAKE A TRIP to fish Yorkshire hill streams on the border between England and Scotland with wet flies. That was the home of the soft-hackled wet. They were allegedly first tied there with feathers plucked from poached birds and silk threads filched from sewing baskets. I don't know how much of that is true, but it provides a romantic ring of petty thievery at the seat of soft-hackle origins.

The first book about tying and fishing the flies was W. C. Stewart's *The Practical Angler,* written in 1857. He fished his three spiders, a light, a medium, and a dark, on casts of at least three flies, often more than that. He didn't say how close he fished them, but somebody else described a day spent with him as twenty-four hours of creeping and crawling. It implies that Stewart sneaked right up onto his trout and fished his flies on short casts.

Stewart was a lawyer. It's possible that both his flies and his tactics were learned from poachers among his clients. It's even possible, though far less likely, that his way of moving along a stream was designed to avoid the eyes of the bailiff and gamekeeper rather than those of trout. We don't know that. We do know that he crept along and that he fished his casts of spiders on short upstream casts in his swift and small hill streams.

That's what I wanted to do, and Stewart's water is where I wanted to do it. But the desire to fish soft-hackles there was instilled not as much by Stewart's fine book as by Sylvester Nemes, whose *The Soft-Hackled Fly* was published in 1975. I read it not long after it came out. I was enthralled by it. Its subject was a few simple soft-hackled wet flies. Its treatment, in perfect keeping with its subject, was short and tightly focused. Its prose—Sylvester, with whom I've now fished many times, is always surprised to hear me say this—was so tuned to his subject and his treatment of his subject that his writing became elegant, not in any flowery way, but in the way that a piece of art becomes beautiful for the way it's so carefully selected to suit its subject.

Sylvester's book led me to Stewart's far older book, and the two of them led to my desire to fish Scotland. But I knew I needed practice before I went over there to fish wet flies upstream. I didn't want to try it cold. So I tied up an Altoids tin full of March Brown Spiders, Partridge and Greens, Partridge and Oranges, Partridge and Yellows, all from Sylvester's book, most in sizes 10 and 12. Some I tied with the prescribed hare's mask fur thorax behind the hackle and some without it. I tucked the tiny tin into my belt bag and carried it whenever I scooted up a small stream. But fishing was largely fine that summer, and I deemed it foolish to take off a working dry fly that was catching trout to try an untried wet. So I neglected my practice.

Then one July day, when the water was low and the sun was bright on one of my favorite coastal hill streams, the trout suddenly became bashful about dry flies. They'd rush at them, boil up under them, splash them, even jump over them. But they refused to take them. I tried a variety of drab and small ones, but the results were the same. I sat down on a boulder, pondered my luck, perused once again the contents of my single dry-fly box, looking for something different that therefore might work. Then I caught sight of that mints tin, full of Sylvester's soft-hackles, still lined up in their undisturbed, tidy rows.

I plucked out a Partridge and Yellow, without fur thorax, in size 10. I nipped off my dry fly and tied on the wet, a formula that I've found works perfectly after years of doing the same thing on waters small and large all over the world: The leader that is tuned to tossing a dry fly is just right for fishing a soft-hackle in the same situation.

The first pool I approached to fish, after I stood up from tying on that fly, was a dark and narrow slot hemmed in between two huge boulders that had peeled off the hillside, tumbled down, and wedged together in the streambed to form a V at the bottom. The sloping sides of the pool were the faces of the two boulders. A waterfall about a foot high formed the head of the plunge pool, so there was no current tongue, just an even current flowing down the length of the entire pool, all of twenty feet long. The sun slanted in at the perfect angle to light the top half of those dark depths, so I was able to see a couple of feet into the water column.

I made my first cast from a position at the tailout of this pool, sending the fly fifteen feet up into the even sheet of currents. The leader landed, as it often does, with a few kinks and coils standing above the surface. I watched these closely, along with the tip of my floating line, though I had no expectation that anything was about to happen. Something did. Before the fly had a chance to drift a foot, those little loops of leader that rode an inch or so above the surface suddenly were gone. They were pulled under so sharply that I could no longer see them but could see the slight disturbance of the surface made when they were pulled through it.

My brain did not need to send my arm a message to set the hook. I yanked the rod up and played a trout leaping down the length of the pool to me, admired it a moment, unpinned the big soft-hackle from its lip, and released it. I expected the lower end of the pool to be ruined by the fight, but I cast again to the same spot and had the same thing happen. Two trout of the same size later, I began to reassess the number of fish I'd always believed each pool might hold. I'd always caught one, at most two, on dry flies before things ended and it was time to move upstream to the next pool. This pool kept providing trout after trout to the soft-hackled wet.

When it was finally over I'd taken six, though they'd by then begun to diminish dramatically in size. Still, fishing that pool with a soft-hackled wet fly was an epiphany, one of the most exciting moments in my small-stream fly-fishing life.

When I got to the head of the pool, at that minor waterfall that formed it, I found myself creeping up behind a big boulder and peering over it into the next pool. This one was shorter but formed in the same way by big boulders. I saw no signs of trout in it but knew there would be lots of lies tucked into crevices and ledges along and beneath the boulders on both sides. The tailout looked good. Rather than cast up into the body of the pool, I crouched out of sight behind that big boulder at the tailout and flicked the soft-hackle just the length of the leader up into the current.

That prompted a revelation. A small cloud of trout rushed from the variety of lies among the boulders and attacked the visible fly. The largest one got it. I was able to see the take; all this was lit by the sun. I was almost able to observe the look of astonishment on the trout's frontal physiognomy when I lifted the rod and set the brakes on the its dash back toward the lie from which it had emerged. The revelation was this: It was a lot more fun watching the actual take to a wet fly drifting along just beneath the surface than it was watching the take to a dry fly farther out, afloat on the surface.

The reason was simple enough then and still is: When a trout rushes a sunk fly that you're fishing within sight, you get to see the trout itself, as well as the take itself, not just the distant splash of the take. That is exciting. I also enjoyed watching the excitement caused by the sudden arrival of the soft-hackle in the waters of a pool. That stream was steep, ideally suited to taking a position right in the drop into the pool I'd just fished. I was able to hide behind boulders and stay out of sight of the pool I was about to fish. I could cast very short and watch not just my line tip or leader but the fly itself, most of the time.

The bright soft-hackle, with its yellow body and hackle of gray partridge, white speckled with black spots, was easy to see. Because it was tied on a dry-fly hook, it sank scant inches, then drifted along at the same level. Its posture was most interesting. You remember Mary Poppins descending over London in the opening scene of the movie, suspended from her umbrella? Take away Miss Poppins, and a soft-hackle adrift on the currents would look precisely like that umbrella. The fly, probably because the hook bend is always heavier than its eye, and because the buoyant leader leads away from the fly up to the surface, took the open, upright position, its splayed hackle up, its body vertical beneath it, the hook bend precisely like the handle of an upright umbrella.

It is often written that the effectiveness of a soft-hackled wet fly is caused by its hackle opening and closing in the currents, making the fly look alive. That's all true when the fly is fished in vigorous water, say a riffle in a bigger trout stream, and on the swing. When fished upstream, in the calm water of a small-stream pool, the fly looked exactly like an open umbrella, held up against rain. It did not *work* in the sense of having any inherent movement. It worked wonders in terms of enticing trout.

The wet fly prompted all sorts of antics from trout that day. I'd see them rush it in a bunch on the first cast to any pool, sometimes five or six of them at a time. The largest would almost always inhale it instantly, before any smaller trout could get to it. I'd play the trout to hand, unpin it, drop it into the pool below me, where I'd already fished. Then I'd cast again, the cloud of trout would appear again, and the next largest trout would take it, though slightly less swiftly. I'd play it out, unhook it, deliver it downstream, cast again, hook another.

When only two or three suspicious trout were left, they'd dash at the fly, come to an abrupt halt half a foot or so from it, stare at it, dart nervously around it. Sometimes one would take it hesitantly. Sometimes they'd all turn and flee from it in horror, as if they'd suddenly seen the truth about it. Sometimes they'd simply fade away. When that happened, one of them would often return to it alone, take it surreptitiously, as if pulling something over on its buddies.

It was all more fun than I'd had on a small stream in a long time. I fish those flies and that method often now. They work better for me as streams get steeper, with more plunge pools, letting me stalk closer to the trout to get a better gander at my fly as it descends the length of a pool. That means I use soft-hackles most often in mountain streams. But they were originated in Scottish foothill streams and first fished over longer riffles, runs, and pools. I've used them on that kind of water as well, always creeping close, casting short, watching the leader and line tip for signs of takes. They work well and take trout. But they don't work any better on that type of water than a nymph dangled beneath a dry fly or fished behind a yarn indicator. Since it's easier to notice takes with those methods, I usually neglect wet flies on that kind of water.

It's a shame because that is the very kind of water I desired to fish when I first began practicing with soft-hackled wets fished upstream, so I'd learn to fish them when I got there. I entered into this fishing with the sense that it was practice for Scotland. I've yet to get there.

I don't do much with wets fished on the swing in small streams. Most small streams are too narrow for me to take up a position at the edge of a pool, cast across, and fish a fly on the swing. To do so successfully, on the few pools large enough that it would work, would require wading downstream so that the initial position could be taken upstream from undisturbed trout. Small streams, as I define them, are almost always too constricted, either by the banks themselves or by brush and trees lining the banks. They do not allow an approach from downstream or movement around each pool to get to its head, in order to fish flies on the swing down and around from there.

These restrictions could all be avoided by entering the stream at the upstream end and fishing downstream. But that would reduce dry-fly fishing, and the upstream nymph, to minor methods. I consider the swung wet a minor method on small streams and almost always fish the way I prefer, moving upstream.

The downstream wet can be effective, however, and it's valuable to know how to fish it when you need it. You might even desire to fish downstream most of the time—every angler delivers a different personality to the waters fished. I've always sworn that I'd spend a week on a small stream, fishing downstream every day, learning all I can about the method. But I've never done that. When I do, it's possible I'll get into revelations like I did when I decided to fish soft-hackled wets upstream. It might be more fun than I think. It's certain to be productive enough, given the right circumstances and enough attention.

Position is very important to fish wet flies downstream, because wet flies are not effective when made to swim strongly straight upstream, against the current. Trout don't see natural insects doing that. Trout are, in my experience, put off by it. That is why a position off to the side of a pool, not directly at its head, is critical. If you're straight upstream and cast straight downstream, the only way you'll catch many trout is to feed slack into the drift, and let the fly follow the current. Then you'll have a tough time telling about takes. That's a very minor method.

I've often tried fishing wet flies straight downstream with little result. I'll tell you why I try it. Whenever I park my rig and hike down a stream any distance from a few hundred yards to a couple of miles, in order to turn around and fish back upstream to the rig, I hit the stream and look at the pools below me and have to go try them. Most of the time, I rig the dry I'm most likely to use when I begin fishing upstream. Sometimes I rig a wet and move down a pool or two, dangling and dapping it in front of me.

It's an old method. I'd like to report that trout love it. I'd be lying, at least from my own experience. I move down carefully, take a position at the head of a pool, keep out of sight, cast short to lay the fly on the current, then feed slack while the fly slides downstream. It should work. It does at times. But most often all I do is spoil the pool on the first cast, because my line follows the fly down and is seen by all trout there.

If the stream is big enough—striding the border between small and medium—that I can move to the side of its pools, then I'll be able to fish it more effectively. It's necessary to creep into position and stay low. The cast should be right into the uppermost current and will obviously be very short. The fly—or brace of them, if you'd like to try two, one small and one large, or one drab and one bright—should be allowed to swing down and around. You'll get a very short swing on most small-stream pools. Let the fly or flies cross the seam between the fast current into which you cast and the slower water to the inside. That's where most strikes will happen.

If nothing happens, pick up and cast again, placing the fly or flies a foot or two downstream from the first swing. Repeat the process. This method begins to work best when you use it to explore the soft currents on both sides of the main center current. You'll need to make many mends or feed lots of slack, all to control the speed of the fly. You'll take trout this way. If you're like me, you'll not enjoy it as much as you would fishing a dry fly or nymph upstream through the same water.

However, some pools are shaped so that upstream methods are restricted. If you approach a pool from downstream, you'll often find decid-uous limbs and conifer boughs sweeping low, preventing an upstream pre-sentation. If you move to the side of the same pool, cast upstream from the same obstructions, and let the current escort a wet or pair of them down under whatever overhangs the pool, you'll fool fish. Sometimes they'll be very nice ones because those sorts of lies offer lots of protection and can be the best lies in the pool, and trout holding in them rarely see flies.

Keep the downstream wet fly in your list of tactics, as a minor method, in case you find a situation that can be solved by it. I'll give you a rare example.

I was fishing with artist Richard Bunse on a tiny stream that flowed through his property in Oregon's central Willamette Valley. A retiree had recently bought the property downstream from him, at once hung a No Trespassing sign from a cable strung across the stream. Bunse, out of desire to stay away from such a cranky neighbor, complied with it. But one of his favorite pools, one he'd fished often in his past, was just forty feet downstream from that damned sign.

The best lie in the pool was below a boulder that almost broke the surface where the current entered the pool and slowed down a bit. A trout always held there. Before the sign went up, Bunse could depend on catching that trout.

I watched him solve this problem. He tied on a Royal Coachman wet fly, got right up under the cable, tipped his rod over for a sidearm cast, and shot his cast thirty feet downstream, tight against the far bank. As the fly drifted downstream toward the boulder, on its far side, Bunse fed it slack, throwing line to follow the fly along the bank. When the wet fly reached a position a couple of feet beyond the boulder, Bunse tipped his rod over in the opposite direction, let the line draw tight, let it coax the fly out away from the bank, right toward the boulder. The line washed over the top of the boulder. The fly swung across just downstream from it. A trout smacked it. Bunse brought it in, looked it over to be sure it was the right one. It was: twelve inches long, a fine cutt that might one day go all the way to the ocean and become a sea-run. Bunse released it back to its lie below the cable.

It's a wet-fly method that can be used to pick trout out of specific difficult lies. I hope you don't need to use it against nasty neighbors.

I've used two-fly rigs quite often on medium and large trout streams. They work well, though not as often to catch two trout at once as to find out what fly trout like best: large or small, bright or drab. But I don't use two flies very often on small streams. The environment has too many other troubles to offer. I don't need to add the risk of constant tangles.

There is a kind of day that I've promised to construct for myself, though I've not yet done it. In theory, it's idyllic. It's this: I'd like to tuck a small novel and a nice lunch into my little canvas belt bag. The lunch would include a bottle of beer, or a half-liter bottle of wine, though that would require a glass, and then things would begin to get complicated. But you know the kind of lunch I mean, one that can be enjoyed slowly, while reading a good book.

I'd park the rig at the stream at midmorning, rig up a wet, fish downstream a couple of hours. Then I'd find a wonderful place to lie in the sun, eat that lunch and read that book. I'd take a nap. When I woke up, I'd tie on a dry fly, fish the same water back up to the rig. I'd like to know which part of that day might be most productive: the wet fished downstream or the dry fished up. It might be the lunch but that would be okay, too.

I don't often fish wet flies in response to specific small-stream hatches. One of my favorite seasons, however, is the September hatch of little green stoneflies, often called olive sallies. These are size 16 and 18, at times even smaller. They crawl around on streamside stones, fall to the water, and get eaten by trout. But my signal to switch to a small Partridge and Green is the sight of them in twos, threes, and rarely in bunches, descending from the sky, ignited like green sparks by the sun, landing on riffles to deposit their eggs.

Trout like wets better than drys when this happens. I like getting so close to the water I've got to be on my knees, casting so short I can see the wink or the turn of a take. It's fun and productive.

I also like to fish a Partridge and Yellow in spring, when sporadic hatches of sulfur duns happen. Trout generally ignore a sulfur dry but take the yellow wet eagerly. I don't know why, but I know it works and is fun.

Alderflies descend in their awkward flights over some streams in late May and June. They're not everywhere. They're not very predictable. When trout take them, they also take wet flies but ignore drys. It's rare, but when it happens, it's nice to be armed for it and to know what to do about it.

That's the small number of flies, and the minor number of tactics, that wet flies amount to for me on small streams. I use them to solve specific situations: bright days when trout splash drys but won't take them, specific hatches when trout feed on adults but take them subsurface, lies downstream from No Trespassing signs. Wet flies are always fun to fish when they work, and they always seem to work when no other types of flies fool fish.

You should carry a few and know when and how to use them.

CHAPTER THIRTEEN

Streamer Situations

IT IS CONSTANTLY WRITTEN THAT STREAMERS WORK BEST IN EARLY spring when the water is high and often unclear. That's a good theory on trout streams from medium size up to large, where it's easy to put a streamer into play with cross-stream casts and downstream swings. On small waters, at least for me, it remains largely a theory. I rarely use streamers when the water is high.

If high water is clear, the air somewhat warm, and trout at least modestly active, I'd rather try setting fairly large dry flies onto tiny patches of still surface at pool corners, upstream and down from mid-stream boulders, on slight dark slicks on the surface that denote trenches in the bottom below. If the water is not clear, or the air is cool, insects are inactive, and therefore trout show no interest in the surface, I'd rather go down after them on the bottom with nymphs. By rigging with an indicator, I'm able to receive news about takes. That's difficult informa-tion to get when you use streamers in the same kinds of conditions.

Most streams that fit my loose and somewhat awkward definition of small are too narrow, in most places, to fish from the edges with cross-stream casts. It's a method that works well, but where it does, I believe you're fishing waters that are medium or even large. On a small stream, you're generally forced to fish either directly upstream into the current or directly downstream with the current. If you fish a heavily weighted streamer with upstream casts on small water and let it bounce back toward you along the bottom during high water, you'll probably get strikes but will not know about many of them. Trout will intercept the fly in its drift, be offended by its taste and texture, and spit it out before you know anything happened. Maybe a streamer should be fished in such a situation with an indicator, as one would a nymph, but I've never tried that and have no reason to think a streamer fished with a nymph rig would be as effective as a nymph fished with a nymph rig.

If you fish a streamer from upstream, casting it down the length of a pool and retrieving it back up, you'll never get it deep enough to interest trout in high water unless you weight it like a bomb. Even then, the firm currents of high water will apply pressure to your line and leader, and likely keep the fly lifted up out of the range of interest of bottom-holding trout. If that were not enough reason against fishing a streamer straight downstream in high water, then consider that trout are not accustomed to seeing baitfish swim mightily upstream directly into strong currents. That sort of unnatural movement turns trout off. I've rarely had anything but curious looks, refusal swirls, and sometimes light curiosity taps when fishing streamers on retrieves straight upstream in any water conditions, high, normal, or low.

I tend to use streamers on small streams when the water is down to normal levels and sometimes even when it's low and clear. I usually use them to prod trout out of the kinds of almost bulletproof lies that I suspect hold big fish, but they refuse to budge for smaller flies. This method arrived to me as a kind of lightning strike, and I think you might like to be struck by it as well.

I was on a small Missouri spring creek, fishing with Dick Ryan and the late Tom Widmar, both of St. Louis. Tom was editor of *Flyfishing Heritage,* a wonderful magazine that had recently failed. I'd written for him but never met him. I found him a delightful character whose sense of humor was somewhat subdued by the setback of his pet project. His humor came out quietly, as did Dick Ryan's. Dick is an insurance agent and had access to this spring creek that ran through the grounds of a Catholic monastery. He took Tom and me there and told us how to rig to fish it.

It was late February, cold as hell. On Dick's advice I rigged a long leader and a small yarn indicator and searched through my fly boxes for a generic nymph. I started to tie on a size 12 Hare's Ear. Dick peered over my shoulder, said, "That's awfully big for this stream, Dave." So I replaced it with a size 16, struggling to tie it on with numb fingers. The air was so frigid that we had to stop fishing every half hour to submerge our rods underwater to get the ice out of the guides.

The stream was shrouded by sycamore trees that would have been beautiful when leafed out in spring and summer. They lowered gnarled branches down protectively over all the small pools and long glides along undercut banks of the tiny stream in winter. Storms had broken off a supply of these branches and dropped them into the water I was trying to fish. When I didn't get my nymph hung up on a branch hanging from overhead, on the cast, I'd catch one or two of them once the fly got into the water, on every drift.

I fished up along the edge of a submerged log, thinking if there was a nice trout anywhere in the stream, it would be back in the darkness beneath it. The nymph dangled along as near to that darkness as I could get it. Nothing came out after it. I moved on upstream.

It was frustrating fishing. After an hour of it, I'd had no hits and had surrendered expectations of any. I used my iced-up guides as an excuse to sit on a fallen log with Tom, a hundred feet or so upstream from the good-looking lie along the submerged sycamore. Tom had loaned me a flannel-lined Barbour jacket and wore one himself. We sat in his black jackets on the log in the wintry sycamore forest and talked about writing—his magazine was all essays, fun to write for—and about fishing.

While we talked, Dick, who had been politely fishing well back behind us, came idling along, arrived at that same submerged log. He cast something out to it, waited a moment, then started a retrieve that was almost instantly interrupted by a slashing strike. He set the hook, played out what looked like a two-pound rainbow as quickly as he could, got it unhooked and back into the water before Tom and I could bound down to see what had happened. When we got there, Dick was trying to hide his fly.

Tom knew Dick a lot better than I did. He said, "Let's have a look at what you're using!"

Dick revealed a size 8 lead-eyed Olive Woolly Bugger. He held his rod out to me, said, "Want to try it, Dave?"

I did. I cast that fly toward the darkness beneath the submerged log. It landed with a smack, sank like a stone, and disappeared in a bright flash before it got two feet beneath the surface. I played the fish out quickly, released it, and jammed my wet hand into the warmth of a jacket pocket. The trout was a rainbow, half the size of Dick's but still a very nice fish for the size stream we were fishing. I asked Dick how many trout he'd caught, coming along behind us.

"Just a few," he said. "Just a few."

It's a tactic I've applied constantly ever since, whenever I find appropriate water on a small stream, no matter what the water conditions or weather. It works consistently and rarely fails to take the largest trout from whatever water it's applied against. I've never changed from the lead-eyed Olive Woolly Bugger that Dick used, because it has always worked for me. It's in the narrow mix of small-stream flies I carry constantly to this day, to use on small waters all over the world.

It's very effective in corner pools, the kind where a little riffle dashes down, bumps against the bank, turns abruptly, leaves a slowly whirling eddy tucked up against whatever sort of bank it bumped against, anything from a boulder wall to a grassy overhang. Sometimes there is foam on top. That foam gathers food and tells about predatory trout below. If the water holds brown trout, plop a weighted streamer right in the middle of that tiny swirl of foam and hold on. Takes won't be gentle.

The method doesn't require the presence of brown trout. I remember one day fishing a half mile or so of lower Slough Creek, in Yellowstone Park, with my good friend Tony Robnett. We worked upstream with dry flies, taking turns fishing the pools and long, grass-edged runs of the tiny stream. It was late summer, a hopper kind of day, and we did very well on trout twelve to fourteen inches long. When we'd got as far as we wanted to get from the rig we rested awhile and watched buffalo browse peacefully in the broad meadows, swishing their funny clubbed tails at flies.

When we got up to head back downstream, I tied on a lead-eyed Olive Woolly Bugger, size 12 because the smaller size is easier to handle on a light rod and fishes as well as a larger one, at least on small water. While we walked along, I occasionally tossed the heavy fly into corner pockets, usually where the water turned against a clay bank and tucked a swirl of foam tight against it. Our progress back to the rig was interrupted just a couple of times, but I recall that the Yellowstone cutts that came out of those corners were at least a couple of inches longer, perhaps half a pound heavier, than any we'd taken earlier on dry flies.

Some days, even excellent dry-fly days, I'll be fishing along contentedly on my home waters, or any others, and will arrive at a deep pool and suddenly get the urge to try a weighted Woolly Bugger. I'm not proud about this. I'd like to be able to overcome it. But it's a way to measure what's really down there, the potential the stream has to provide a large trout. I'm not a big-fish fisherman. If I was, I suppose I'd be writing a different sort of book. But I get prodded, at times, to see what sort of trout a stream might hold.

If a stream is tiny, a dry fly will measure its potential as surely as a streamer might. If the stream has deep and hidden depths, however, probing them with a fly of modest size but immodest weight will often prove that larger trout live there than you thought. They'll rarely be much larger, but the average trout you take on a streamer, as opposed to the average trout you take on a dry, might make you realize the stream is a bit better than you thought it was. I'm not recommending you do this. Small streams are too much fun when fished with dry flies. You'd never want weighted streamers to become a habit. But I'd not like to fish a small stream without a small sampling of them to fall back on.

I've found a fairly rare but important application for lightly weighted streamers, usually Muddler Minnows, on small streams. They're not for the depths, instead they are for the shallows. They're not for seasons when the water is high, rather for moments when the water is low, clear, and slow.

Usually it's mid to late summer, or even early autumn, when groundwater has been wicked off and the stream has diminished, with its flows not just well within its banks but thin over spreading pools, at the edges, and in tailouts. Most aquatic insect hatches are over. Trout depend for their living on what I've already described as brush hatches: returns of aquatic insects to lay their eggs or falls of terrestrials from grasses, shrubs, and overhanging trees.

When the main supply of meals shifts from emerging aquatic insects delivered down the currents to all sorts of insects falling to the surface of the water, trout back down from their lies at the heads of pools. They take up positions at the edges or on the thin tailouts. From there they can keep their eyes on a broader bit of surface. They can dash forward to accept anything that lands on what they've established as their territories. It's a distribution of fish that is revealed by V-wakes arrowing up into pools every time you approach the foot of a pool and begin to fish it in the normal way, with casts from the lower end up toward the current tongue that normally defines the lies of most of the pool's trout.

When trout are distributed in the thinnest water at the edges and on the tailout, they become very difficult to catch with the conventional upstream approach. They spook at the sight of you. They flee if they see your line or leader flying over their heads. You move into position to fish what you deem to be the best holding water and discover before you can cast to it that you've spoiled the pool by sending trout out from under your feet, dashing in panic up into the water you are about to fish. Even if trout are up there, they'll catch the panic and ignore your flies.

I've found some success in these situations by fishing dry flies or small nymphs upstream, from crouched positions downstream from the tailout. The cast must be short and delicate. You must almost always drape the line and leader over rocks in the tailout and lay just two to three feet of tippet onto the water. The abrupt arrival of the fly can still spook these trout. When they hold in such shallow water, they're on hair triggers. Anything out of the ordinary will fire them out of there.

It creates a rare opportunity to fish streamers from upstream, but the water must be shaped right for it or the method won't work. It works best where the stream gradient levels out, where pools spread out. I've found such water most often in the freestone reaches of hill streams, least often in the mountains, and surprisingly rarely in meadow streams, where small waters, on account of steady flows, tend to dig narrower, deeper courses.

Where pools spread out and trout hold at the edges and on tailouts, it's possible to approach from upstream, take up a position crouched at the same corner you'd normally expect to fish from downstream, and use a streamer to probe the edges and tailout with casts made across and down. But you can't just sail the fly out there and let it land with a whap on top of trout holding in four to six inches of water. You'll see nothing but those damning arrows, sometimes dashing in all directions until the entire pool gets upset by your first cast.

You must deliver your fly some distance—at least two to at most six feet—from the suspected lie of the trout you'd like to catch. It must land softly enough not to alarm them but, in a perfect world, with enough disturbance to attract their attention and arouse their urge for acquisition. If a trout does not rush the fly right away, you must be patient; let the current slowly deliver it into their sight before you begin to retrieve it. It's in that wait that the method usually fails, and it's not your fault. In water where it works best, edge and tailout currents are usually slow to almost still.

You try to place the fly far enough from trout so that its arrival does not frighten them. Then you wish for the fly to drift close enough for them to see it. But the currents, given the low-water conditions in which trout take up stations lower down in pools, are almost always too slow to deliver the fly in any sort of modern time frame. I don't know if you've read Ray Bergman's fine 1938 *Trout*. If not, you should. This is one of those situations where he might make his cast, light a cigarette, smoke it down, begin his retrieve. If you can do that, this method will suit you. I don't smoke.

So I try to strike a balance, casting downstream toward shallow water where I think trout might hold, giving the fly some time to amble closer to them, then retrieving it out. Half the time I fudge, cast too close, and spook the trout on the cast. Half the time I get impatient and begin the retrieve before trout can get the fly in their sights. Half the time . . . well, I'm out of halves. A very few times, in a very few places, I'm able to catch trout with this method.

One of my favorite places for it is a long bench where one of my home hill streams levels out and loses its urgency. Its pools spread out over gravel because the slow current speed allows deposition of finer material than speeds upstream or down, where the current is faster and the bottom tends to be bouldered. The stream is overshadowed by a high alder canopy. As soon as mayfly and stonefly hatches trickle to an end in early summer, trout turn to caddis and terrestrials that arrive by air and land more often than by water.

Gathering currents over the graveled tailouts form perfect habitat for sculpins. They hold along the bottom, perfectly camouflaged among small stones, feed on insects, make short dashes from lie to lie. I haven't done many autopsies on this section of stream, but my guess is that trout there are as interested in sculpins as they are in any insects that might land on the pools from overhead.

The pools are fifteen to twenty feet wide in their centers and con-strict down from that width to ten feet or so in the shallows just upstream from the narrow riffles that shuttle the stream into the next pool below. Trout hold in water inches deep along the rim of that semi-circle of gathering flow. A Muddler cast down there to one edge, allowed to sink, then brought slowly across the tailout on the swing will draw V-wakes to it rather than send them bolting away from it.

The method works there because the current of the tailouts delivers the fly into the range of the trout without the need to smoke a cigarette after each cast, before beginning each retrieve. It still requires patience, but not more than I'm able to provide. Part of my lack of hurry in that place is because the picture is so beautiful. I'm always crouched near the head of the pool or on my knees on fine gravel, overhung by alders, struck by sunshine filtering through the leaves, able to gaze off at all that beauty around me while the fly sinks and is pushed downstream. I usually make a downstream mend to enable the current to pick up the speed of the drift a bit.

That downstream mend also puts the line in the perfect position from which to initiate the retrieve. When the line has floated downstream far enough to begin getting tugged by the tailout itself, then it animates the fly. That's when I draw my attention in from the scenery and watch for anything arrowing after the fly. It doesn't happen on every cast. It doesn't happen in every pool. But it happens often enough to keep me happy and in that prayerful position on my knees. And it's the only way I've been able to solve some of those pools.

The cutts that come out of them are not mighty, rarely more than ten to twelve inches long. Their colors and slender shapes are in perfect keeping with where they live. I always promise myself that I'm going to keep a couple of them, kill them for those autopsies I'd always like to perform to confirm my theories about sculpins and cook them with butter and sliced scallions over an open fire right there alongside the stream. But when I get one in my hands, I'm never able to snap its neck.

Some small meadow streams get shaped almost perfectly for fishing with streamers. They flow narrowly between willow-grown banks, gouge deep pools beneath the willow roots at all their bends. The ones I'm thinking about—nameless, I'm ashamed!—hold brown trout that get bigger than they ought to in such small water. But their food, some of which comes swimming, more of which falls off the banks, arrives in large bites and plentiful supply.

The one I enjoy most, flowing across a broad flat in public land right out in the middle of Montana, fishes best with streamers at the end of warm days. The last time I was there was filled with reward, and some of the most beautiful sights I've ever seen while fishing for trout, but for trout held in the hands it ended nearly empty.

It started in a rush. A couple of friends and I were driving by, in late afternoon, on our way somewhere else. But we'd be driving in the night before we got where we were going, and here was this stream very near us. We'd fished it often enough in our pasts to know we'd be fools to not stop. So we did. By the time we'd sorted our gear, tugged on waders, and strung up rods, it was only a couple of hours before night would fall. We galloped to the water and split in different directions. I didn't see anybody else until we'd gathered back at the rig in the dark. But I heard continual shouting from other parts of the willow flat through which the stream meandered.

I did some shouting of my own, most in minor agony.

I rigged a dry and beadhead dropper first and tried fishing it upstream along the edges. Nothing came to either fly in the first bend pool. When I tried to wade around the inside of the corner up to the next pool, I discovered that the current was pushy enough, in that constricted channel, to make wading not dangerous, just difficult. I got there, though, and tried the dry and dropper rig again. Nothing came to it again.

The pools were deep; there was foam at some corners; I knew there were browns in the stream, so I tied on a heavily weighted Olive Woolly Bugger, size 6 or 8, and cast it up to the corner I'd just fished with a dry and dropper. A trout came out the instant the fly hit the water, jumped right over the fly, and would have come down on it and taken it if I hadn't jerked it out of there. I have no idea why brown trout do that, but I know it's unnerving, at least to me. I cast up there again, the trout pounced the fly, thrashed once, and dove back under the willow roots from which it had arisen, taking the fly with it. I drew my leader in and looked forlornly at the little pigtail at its end: damning evidence of a knot tied in too much of a hurry.

I tied on another Woolly Bugger, turned and fished slowly downstream, letting the current ease me along, pushed by it rather than fighting it. For the last hour of light, trout after trout rushed out of the edges, leaped after my fly. Sometimes they tossed it; sometimes it tossed them; sometimes I broke them off. Once in a while I caught one, but it was usually one of the smaller ones, a pound or so. One I saw in the air must have weighed three pounds. That's a nice trout from small water. I'd like to have caught it, but I didn't.

When I got back to the rig, I found out that most of the shouting I'd heard from other parts of the willows was about the same thing as mine: more over trout in the air or trout lost than about trout brought to hand. We sat in lawn chairs in the gravel at the back of the rig, taking down rods, taking off waders, getting ourselves ready for the long drive through the rest of the night. We did a lot of laughing.

Nobody complained about all the trout we'd failed to catch.

CHAPTER FOURTEEN

Stalking Beaver Ponds

QUITE OFTEN DURING THE COURSE OF A DAY SPENT EXPLORING UP A small stream, you'll bump into a beaver pond or even a series of them. They will most likely be found far up into the headwaters, where flows have diminished to those the size that beaver can block. If you're on a mountain or foothill stream, you'll almost always find these ponds on benches, where the bounding course of the stream flattens out and slows down. On a meadow stream they might be almost anywhere, but not often where the stream is large enough to have a very forceful flow, and never far out into the open, away from trees.

It's rare that you'll find beaver ponds in anything but constricted conditions. Even on small streams in arid country, beaver usually do their work in willow-lined bottoms. You don't have to search far for the reasons—the succulent saplings entice beaver there in the first place. You don't get to fish many beaver ponds with open, uncrowded banks because such barren banks, though beneficial for your fishing, would not offer beaver anything to eat. Nor would these busy engineers find the materials from which to construct their dams.

Your expectations for trout of any size will dwindle as you move up a small stream toward the types of headwaters where you might find beaver dams. Quite often beaver ponds go unfished because they're separated by a stretch of water, from a few hundred yards to a mile or more long, where the trout are too small to bother pestering. You fish upstream. The water gets smaller and choked in by brush, more difficult to fish. The trout you take from it become tiny. You fish one last pool, lose a couple of flies trying to get one onto the water, finally thread a perfect cast right to where you want it, and a four-inch trout, the monster of the pool, comes up to whack it.

You release that last tiny trout, hook your fly into its keeper, take one wistful look upstream to where the stream disappears into an even more fearful tangle, and turn back downstream. Unless you've done some map research, have heard some rumors, just have a strong hunch, or own an overwhelming curiosity about what might be up there, you're smart to turn around. Many, if not the majority, of small streams lack fishable beaver ponds in their headwaters.

But those that do can suddenly reverse the size of your expectations when you emerge from the brush and stumble onto their expanded waterscapes. If the ponds you find have any size, depth, and constancy of water, they're likely to hold the largest trout in the entire watershed.

I recall the first time I discovered beaver ponds in the headwaters of a stream I'd fished four or five times a season for many seasons. I had fished it for so long that I had a last fishable pool staked out. It was small and hemmed in by alders, but I was always able to get a dry fly onto its water and extract a trout of eight inches or so, the *legal* minimum then, even though that didn't matter because I didn't intend to keep it. Upstream from that pool the stream steepened, becoming far more difficult to navigate. I'd never caught a trout that met my minimum desires in any of the plunge pools that went from there on up into the forest, seemingly forever.

An elk trail crossed the stream at that last good pool. That trail was my delivery straight up a ridge through a few hundred yards of heavy timber to an old cat road, which I could then hike a couple of miles back to my rig, parked where I'd started. I was normally exhausted by the time I reached that last pool. Faced by that hike, I was always ready to reel up and quit.

One day I arrived at the pool early and fresh, I have no idea why, and full of curiosity about what might lie upstream. I cut off my fly, reeled up my line, and broke down my rod. Rather than hike up the elk trail to the cat road, I worked my way a hundred yards or so into the timber, then began following out a tangled network of elk and deer trails and I think at times even squirrel trails, that paralleled the stream.

In places it was a beautiful upright hike through mature conifer forest. In other places it was a hellish struggle through shin-tangles of peckerpoles. A mile of it took a couple of hours, wore me out, and made me sweat. I was beginning to become claustrophobic from the lack of light down inside that deep conifer forest when suddenly I burst out into a broad, bemeadowed opening. A herd of elk stared at me wild-eyed, blew out of there, crashing into the forest on the other side of the meadow. A shot rang out. I thought I'd interrupted a poacher at his work.

It turned out I'd startled the elk during the napping and cud-chewing part of their day. Their thrashing flight had frightened a beaver into smacking the water with its tail. That sent a flock of mallards splashing and quacking frantically into the air at the upper end of the meadow. The first time I arrived at that little string of beaver ponds, it was not in peace, but in pandemonium.

I did not have the brains or the patience to sit and let things settle. I rushed out to the broadened water, falling into beaver holes, scrambling back out of them, trying to string my rod and scout the water and navigate an obstacle course all at the same time. I jumped up onto the dam, which in itself would have sent half the trout sailing to the opposite end of that first pond, had they not already been crouched in fear from the commotion made by the elk, beaver, and mallards. I fumbled on the same big dry fly I'd been casting over the water I'd fished in the stream up to my traditional last pool.

Trout, if they were in that pond, did not reveal themselves or express any interest in the fly I was fishing. Rather than wait for calm to restore itself, I rushed around the pond, cut through a narrow band of alders and willows, and discovered a second beaver pond upstream from the first. This one was hemmed in more narrowly by trees. I came out of them quietly and stood watching the water, not because I'd managed to slow myself down, but because I could see no place from which to launch a cast without hooking something behind me rather than in front of me.

The pond was no more than fifty feet from end to end, half that wide. While I surveyed it, not for trout, but for a place from which I might cast and hit the water, I saw a swirl in the shallows where what was left of the stream leaked in at the upper end of the pond. That disturbance in the water was made by something bigger than anything I'd ever caught in the main part of the stream now a mile of forest behind me.

I'd like to say I made a brilliant cast and caught it, but that would be a lie. I backed into the alders, forced my way through them to the head of the pond, emerged out of the tangle there, and found no place from which I could launch as much as a roll cast. I tried stepping into the water to get free of the brush, but my foot went into muck, and the violence of extracting it sent waves all over the pond and a startled wake shooting down toward the dam. That was that for that pond.

I found another, smaller, even more hemmed in, upstream. I didn't see any fish in it, nor any way to fish for them if they were there. The brush opened out; a smaller meadow pond widened the bit of stream that was left; and then the stream tipped up and entered forest again. In that last open pool, not as big as some of the pools in the larger part of the stream far down toward where I'd started fishing hours earlier, I hooked and landed a foot-long cutt, as large as any I'd caught all day.

By the time I returned to the first pond, away from which I'd frightened the herd of elk, the surface was calm and two or three trout were rising. I slipped to the tiny delta at its head, crouched in the bunchgrass there, waited until a trout rose within range, and set my fly about five feet to the near side of its rise rings. I'd waited so long I was about to lift the fly and cast it ten feet farther out when the fly disappeared in a sudden swirl. That trout was larger than any I'd caught in all the years I fished the stream, which is the way it often happens when you fish beaver ponds.

An admonition: Don't kill them. It's easy to clean a beaver pond out of a season's worth of its catchable trout, though the incoming stream will almost always provide spawning and therefore replenishment in seasons to come.

Getting into a good position from which to cast without frightening fish is almost always the largest problem when fishing beaver ponds. Sometimes the best place to stand is on the dam itself, but be sure you can use it without doing any damage. Breaking down a dam is not fatal to it; beaver will repair it. But if it's summer or fall and flows are low, it might take so long for repairs and subsequent refilling that all the trout in the pond die before there's enough water for them to thrive once again.

Even if you can kneel on a beaver dam and fish with a clear backcast and forecast area, you'll usually have to work with truncated casts. All the protruding sticks and debris of a beaver dam are sure to catch any line that you drop at your feet, so you can only cast what you can hold in your line hand. It sounds easy, especially if you're a salmon or steelhead fisherman, accustomed to holding loops of line in your hand. But let me assure you, if you cast from a beaver dam, you're going to curse what you're standing upon.

The best position I've found for approaching and fishing the best water in beaver ponds is just downstream from the dam. Creep right up to it. Keep low and let the dam hide you from any trout cruising or holding just upstream from it. That's often the location of the deepest water in the pond and, therefore, the address of the largest trout in the pond. Make your first casts, whether you're fishing a floating or sunk fly, to the water just on the other side of the dam from where you're hiding. It's often your best chance to take a trout or two. It's also often your best chance to get all tangled up, with your fly line lying across the same branches and debris that would tangle up your slack if you were standing on top of the dam. That's life on beaver ponds. If they were not tangled, beaver and trout would not be there.

The next most likely position is at the head of a pond, where the incoming stream inserts itself. The reason is almost the same: The inflowing stream clears its own channel and is likely to create room for a backcast. Where it does, you'll probably need to move into position at a crouch and fish from your knees, because you'll have no dam to hide behind. If clumps of grass, shrubs, or a lone tree form cover you can use as a blind, while still being able to cast, use it.

If the pond is tiny, you might be able to cover all of it from these two positions, fishing from atop or behind the dam first, then moving up to fish from the head. If it's larger, you'll have to find additional casting positions around the edges. On a typical pond, this is not easy. Some have floating logs. These are excellent launching platforms for casts, but be sure to fish your way out along them before getting up and walking them. The most likely place for pond trout to hold is right under the log you'd like to walk to get out to where you can cast. Explore both sides of it, ahead of yourself, as you edge your way out.

You'll often have to do this with roll casts because you'll find no room for a backcast. That is true for many of the positions you'll be forced to take around the rim of the average beaver pond. You'll be inserted into brush, and a backcast would be fatal. Roll casting might be your only option around the entire circumference of many ponds.

Some ponds are so brushy and break off so steeply from the edge right into modestly deep water, that even getting room to roll-cast can be a problem. In such a case you might be able to take a wading position. Be careful about muck. Sometimes you step into what looks like shallow water and find that you're mired. If it doesn't become dangerous to you, your thrashing to get out will reduce your danger to trout.

I've fished beaver ponds where the only way to get into position to make a reasonable cast was to slip along the trunks of fallen trees submerged along the bottom. This sort of wading and fishing is a prescription for misadventure. You tiptoe along or slide your feet right down the center of the log. You stop to take a few casts where a branch or two join the trunk and give you footholds that allow some balance. Then you see a rise you can't reach, and you leave your secure position, moving out farther, where the trunk you're following gets thinner, deeper, and more depressed into the mucky bottom.

I don't need to describe the ending of that trip; you're the one out there. Good luck getting back.

Fishing dry flies on small ponds is mostly a matter of placing the flies over rises. If there's a consistent rise, it's a good idea to notice what trout might be taking. If rises are sporadic, which is more likely the case, then it's probable that a generic dry fly will work fine. Trout on ponds see quite a variety of things, just as trout in small streams see both aquatic and terrestrial insects landing on their waters. The same drys that work in the stream leading up to the pond will often work on the pond itself. The problem is more likely to be position and presentation than matching any hatch.

But if a hatch is happening, do your best to observe it and at least approximate it. That's why you carry those searching flies that are based on trout food forms: the Elk Hair for caddis, Stimulator for stoneflies, Parachute Hopper for grasshoppers, which can be victims of trout in the uncommon meadow pond. I don't use the Adams much on small streams because its drab colors make it too difficult to see. But I always carry a few for the beaver pond I might encounter in the course of a day spent on a small stream. It has the common mayfly shape. Its gray body, mixed grizzly and brown hackle and tail, and grizzly hackle–tip wings make it look like a lot of things that either emerge from ponds or land on their surfaces. It works. In size 14 or so, it is the first dry fly I usually try on a beaver pond, if I see occasional rises but nothing specific to imitate.

When trout are rising sporadically, it's best to place your dry fly as gently as you can a foot or two to the near side of any rise you can reach. If you get it there soon enough, chances are the trout hasn't moved far away and will see the fly arrive. By casting short of the rise, you reduce the chance that the trout will see your line and leader in the air. If all it notices is the sudden presence of the fly lighting on the water, the trout is likely to rush up and grab it before any of its friends see it.

It's most fun to fish drys on beaver ponds when trout are cruising and rising with predictable movements. You might see a rise, then another a few feet away. If it's the same trout and you place your fly in line with the rises and ahead of the fish, you know what will happen next. Be patient on the hook set. Anticipation might cause you to blow the fly out of there the instant you see that nose begin to emerge.

At rare times I've seen trout in beaver ponds cruise in repeated circular or oval paths. They're like walkers circling the high school track for exercise, except they're conserving energy and looking for food. Every few feet they dart for something subsurface or nose up to examine something in the surface. Then they resume course. They're not usually feeding selectively when they do this. You can almost always catch a trout set up in such a pattern by waiting until it goes past your position, then casting your dry fly where you know the trout's habit will take it. You'll be able to see it coming. You'll see the instant it notices your fly, takes interest in it, shifts course slightly to examine it, and tips up to take it. Restrain yourself.

You can enjoy some success with dry flies even when no trout are rising. Most beaver ponds are somewhat shallow. Most beaver pond trout cruise slowly, on the watch for whatever food they can find. If you cast a dry fly out and let it sit, especially if it's near some sort of cover or over a submerged weed bed, any trout that sees it might be glad to get it. Don't invest a lot of time in this kind of blind fishing. If you fish drys for more than half an hour and don't get a hit, it's time to switch to something sunk.

That's usually a wet fly for me, an Alder or Leadwing Coachman in size 12 or 14, or a generic nymph, a Hare's Ear or Fox Squirrel a size or two smaller, usually size 16 or 18. The leader should be about the same length as the one you used for the dry fly, which should be the one you've been using on the stream down below, with the possible addition of a couple feet of tippet one size finer than what you were using when you fished the faster water. That serves to both lengthen and fine down your leader, both advantages when you change from fishing moving water to stillwater.

If I'm using a wet fly, I'll cast in a fan-shaped arc from my initial position in order to cover all likely water. I'll let the fly sink a bit. Since I don't carry a wet-tip line when fishing small streams, I'll be using the floater, and the fly will never get more than a few inches deep. But that's often enough with a wet fly. My retrieve will be the standard short strip with the line hand, sometimes with some staccato twitching of the rod tip added. Beaver pond trout are almost always opportunistic and usually hungry. I have great luck with them on wet flies.

I like wets for their slow sink rate and shallow running depth. Beaver ponds often have myriads of submerged twigs, sticks, and stumps. These all form likely lies for trout or likely focal points for cruising and feeding trout. A wet fly can be cast just beyond them and retrieved back past them. Because wets don't sink far they'll usually come back without getting snagged. But a trout holding or moving anywhere around the cover will notice them and rarely let them get away. Once a trout hits, then the adventure of keeping it out of whatever it was that sheltered it gets under way. That doesn't always end well, but it's always fun.

If I want to fish a bit deeper, I'll rig a nymph, usually one that has some weighting wire wrapped around the hook shank. The rig remains the same: a 9- to 10-foot leader tapered down to 4X or 5X. The fan of casts remains the same as well. But after each cast, the fly is given more time to sink. If the pond has some depth, the countdown method can come into play, though with a floating line, giving the fly much more than fifteen or twenty seconds seems to be a waste of patience.

Using a slow hand-twist retrieve is rarely a waste of time when you use a nymph on a beaver pond. I've found that the speed of the retrieve is quite often the key to success. If you've never tried repeating some little mantra between twists, give it a try. Some folks count, but I can't do that. I'll make up a little sentence, different on any given day, say it after each slow twist that brings in another creeping bit of line, and repeat it before beginning the next twist. You can make up your own sentence. If it reflects a positive thought, you'll catch more trout.

A good one might be: The slower the retrieve, the faster the fishing.

If a beaver pond has some size, or if there is a line of ponds strung out along a small stream and for some reason I want to cover them quickly, I'll explore them with an Olive Woolly Bugger, size 10 or 12, lightly weighted. I fish it blind, casting to whatever water I can reach as I move from the dam up along one edge of the pond to the upper end. If I catch a satisfying number of trout, that slows me down. That doesn't seem to bother me.

I use the same Olive Woolly Bugger in small streams that are strung out in pools that are almost ponded. I got onto a tiny tailwater stream once in fall out in the eastern Oregon desert, after summer irrigation flows had been shut down. The water had dropped abruptly, leaving a series of deep, willow-lined pools connected by trickles of riffles. I noticed the similarity of the situation to what beaver might do on the same size stream with the same gentle gradient. It prompted me to tie on the Woolly Bugger, kneel next to the water, cast that fly out, give it some time to sink before beginning a stripping retrieve.

The trout that climbed all over the fly must have been hungry. They were outsize for the water they were in. They were rainbows, with deep bodies and wide red stripes down their sides. A couple of them weighed close to four pounds.

They tore up that small stream, limited my take to one per pool. But that was all right. I was satisfied to catch one, admire it, release it, and move on. It propelled me to explore the stream and exploring is at least half of the reason that I love to fish small streams.

The other half is all the trout I catch.

AFTERWORD
ONE MORE FLY

I JUST RETURNED FROM A JUNE TRIP TO JAPAN, MOST OF IT SPENT traveling and fishing in the northern half of Honshu, the main island. It's mostly mountainous country. Rivers and larger streams in the populated and developed valleys are not precisely pristine, but their feeders in the hills are all small streams. Pretty and densely forested, the small streams provide some surprisingly good trout fishing.

We stayed in Furukawa with Migaku Saito, who builds sweet-casting bamboo fly rods under the name Old Crab. He's far from a crab himself. One day he drove us out for two or three hours, on winding and overcrowded roads, to a favorite stream. It was clean, its water clear as air, its bottom polished gravel and granite boulders. I turned over a few streambed stones. It was rich with the same variety of aquatic insects—clinger and crawler mayfly nymphs, several stonefly species, and cased caddis—that might inhabit a Rocky Mountain stream, though they clearly belonged to different taxonomic genera. A few duns, small stoneflies, and adult caddis emerged out of the water or the brush during the day—not enough to constitute a hatch but enough to keep trout interested in the surface, just as on any small stream on our own continent.

Saito-san never did fish ahead of Masako and me. He always waded along behind, gave us the good water, watched while we fished it, applauded when we extracted 7- to 10-inch *iwana* (spotted char) or *yamame* (residualized males of the cherry salmon) from the pools with our dry flies. These trout are similar in shape and behavior to our brookie and rainbow, though both, perhaps due to an approximate ten thousand years of fishing pressure, were much more bashful about flies. They'd rush them and quite often take them. But they'd spit them out in an instant, necessitating quick hook sets. If they missed the take, or we missed the strike, they'd dash off wildly and never come back.

I looked back once and noticed that Saito-san was off to one side of the stream, behind us, kneeling close to a bit of pocket water pushed up against the edge of a cliff, releasing a trout. Masako and I had both passed up that minor hesitation in the current in our rush to get to a much bigger and prettier pool just above it. It was her turn to fish, and she'd taken a couple of fair-sized fish, so we were happy and pushed on. But I glanced back more and more often after that.

Saito-san stooped to release more and more trout from those tiny pockets that Masako and I passed up. It didn't take me long to notice that a few of his were bigger than any of ours. He explained that there was far more fishing pressure on his stream than on most of ours; the big trout in the best lies all get caught. In Japan, that means they get killed and eaten. So the biggest trout remaining in the stream reside in small pockets that get passed up by most anglers, who like Masako and me head to the prettier and to all appearences more productive pools. Japanese streams have steep gradients, so there are plenty of pools. But there are also plenty of pockets between the pools.

Rather than begin fishing these pockets right away, I dropped back and began watching Saito-san fish them. Earlier in this book I mentioned that the best small-stream fisherman I ever waded with was Etsuo Kikuchi, from Hokkaido, the northern island. Saito-san is just as good. That makes two. That doesn't mean we don't have small stream fishermen over here who are as good or better; it merely reflects the fact that I fish small streams alone most often here and, therefore, fish with few who might be experts, but I need somebody to take me fishing there. But there is little trout fishing in Japan except on small streams. If an angler has fished for thirty or forty years over there, it's all been done on small waters—quite a bit of time for waters to shape skills.

The first thing I noticed about the way Saito-san fished was the nearness of his approach to any lie he expected would hold trout. He moved to it slowly, approaching from one side or other, and got to within ten to fifteen feet. Then he cast, obviously short, and immediately high-sticked his dry fly from the head of the pocket to its tail just as I might fish a nymph. I'd have fished the same water from downstream, perhaps slightly off to one side or the other, and from a bit farther off, with fifteen- to twenty-foot casts: far from long, but about double the distance at which he fished it.

It didn't seem to mean much at first. He fished his way; I would do fine fishing the same water my way. But it occurred to me there was far more to it than that. He solved the problem of the pocket water with position. I solve the same problem with casting. I've admitted earlier in the book that I enjoy the act of casting. Perhaps I like it too much. Fly casting is pure grace when the line is in the air. But small-stream trout are fooled by drag-free drifts, not by the graceful curves of the line in the sky.

By getting up close to the water he was about to fish, Saito-san was able to execute perfect drag-free drifts of his dry fly the length of every pocket he fished, on nearly every cast he made. From my distance, I'd get plenty of perfect drifts, but if I got one on the first cast, it might be an accident. And you know how trout react when a dry fly is racing along, tugged by the line and leader, the first time they see it. They refuse to ever look at it again. So the true value of Saito-san's close approach was a first drift that was consistently just right. The first time any trout would see his fly, it would be floating along as if unattached to leader or line.

In larger pools, the kind of water Masako and I fished that day, position is important. But trout can see out, so casting is equally as important as position—you need to stay back from them far enough to be out of their sight. On frothed pocket water, so common on bounding streams and so limiting to the vision of trout holding in it, position is clearly more important than casting. That's a thought to leave you with—the relative importance of position and casting on different types of small-stream lies. But I'd rather depart from you with another observation, an observation about the fly Saito-san used to probe those pocket lies.

It was a parachute pattern, size 14, with a dark dun tail and hackle, rusty brown body, and a short white puff of lambs' wool for the wing post. That surprised me. I would expect wool to absorb water and sink, especially after it had been washed to whiteness and therefore deprived of its natural lanolin. But his did not because he dressed it with floatant. Many times the fly sank in the rough pocket water as I watched him fish it, but then, as soon as it got past whatever caused it to sink, it popped to the surface again and continued its float. The fly fished fine in that rough water but was not easy to see.

Perhaps Saito-san got so close to his water and fished his fly on such short casts so he could follow its float and notice when a trout took it. If that's the reason for fishing so close it was a good one, but I tried getting up close to the water and fishing my old favorite flies with the same intensity without enjoying similar success.

That night he showed me how to tie his fly. The secret is fine wool, tied fairly thick and clipped short after the fly is finished, so it's a puff more than a wing. Fine white polypro yarn might work as well. Saito-san gave me a piece of the wool on the hide, apparently a lifetime supply. He buys it in the airport on fishing trips to New Zealand, where it is sold as souvenirs or dusters. I took a small sample of his flies, shared them with Masako, and she and I drove north for some further fishing with other friends. By the time we got to where we were going we were calling the nameless fly the Saito-san Special.

I got down to just one of them left on that next trip, having lost all the others to eager trout. I was reluctant to tie that last one on, so I reverted to some of my own favorites, including the Parachute Adams, which looked enough like the Saito-san Special that I expected the same results. I didn't get them. For whatever strange reason, the trout desired that fly and no others that I carried. Finally I relented, tied the last one on, and at once began catching trout again. As we fished up the small stream, we came to a sign strung over some pocket water pools on a cable about fifteen feet in the air overhead. I asked Masako to translate the Japanese.

"It says that it's catch and release from here on up," she told me.

I moved upstream from the sign, made a cast, and had a swift strike at the fly. I missed the hook set, blew the fly out of there, and hooked the cable behind me. Masako laughed at the irony of it: me standing there shaking my rod fruitlessly, about to lose my last taking fly to a catch and release sign. I was not able to laugh with her.

She had a couple of Saito-san Specials left but was losing them to trout at a rate that didn't make her willing to share one of the last ones with me. I couldn't blame her for that. I tried more flies from my own small-stream box. None worked well. I ended the day taking photos of Masako catching trout until she ended her own day by breaking off her last Saito-san Special on a very nice trout.

Now I'm home. I've been tying the fly and using it exclusively on my own small streams. I've been doing extremely well with it, though I'm still not sure whether it's because the fly is better than others or I need to cast it short in order to follow its floats and, therefore, fish it more carefully. It might be a combination of the two. Until I take the time to fish it against my old favorites—the Royal Wulff, Deer Hair Caddis, Parachute Adams—on my favorite waters, I won't know. My guess is my favorites will work as well as they ever have in the same situations in which I've used them in the past, and the Saito-san Special will work no better but will perhaps solve some pocket water problems better than I solved them in the past.

Meantime, I've felt compelled to add a dozen of them to my small-stream selection. Because my one small-stream fly box had no expansion gaps left, I've had to buy another to put them in. I'm carrying two fly boxes now, one full to bursting, the other almost empty. That leaves me with almost an entire box of expansion gaps. You know I'll find flies to fill them.

I don't know if that's good or bad.

INDEX

A

Adams
    classic, 79, 151–152
    Midge, 81
    Parachute, 78–79, 80–81
Alders, 89, 152
Anglers, shaped by streams, 11–18
Angler's Astoria, An (Hughes), 40
A. P. Black, 87
Attractors, 76

B

Backcast, 49
Backwaters, 6
    sites for trout, 64–65
Beaver ponds, 146–154
Beetle Bug, 107
Belt bag
    canvas, 24
    Wood River Sidekick II, 22, 23
Belt packs, 23

Bergman, Ray, 143
Body, pool, 61
Boots, 30–31
Boulders, trout around, 70
Brooks, Charlie, 87, 124
Brook trout, 93, 94
Brown trout, 93, 94
Brush hatches, 92, 141
Bunse, Richard, 134–135

C

Casting
    approaching upstream, 94–95
    backcast, 49
    basic, 49–51
    in bouldered tailouts, 95, 96–97
    control, 46
    in current tongue, 97–101
    curve, 99
    drag, handling, 96, 99, 102–103
    in eddies, 102–104